PRAISE

"Christendom has seen a resurgence of apologetics in the past generation, led in no small measure by the tireless efforts of scholars, like Professor Quist, who have wisely seen that the incarnational and cross-centered focus of Lutheran theology provide a most sure foundation for a factually verifiable proclamation of Christ and Him crucified. This volume presents proof to a legal certainty that indeed 'these things were not done in a corner' but are instead founded on 'many infallible proofs' that have convinced a legion of skeptics of the truth of Christian claims."

—*Craig Parton, AB, MA, JD, Trial Lawyer and United States Director of the International Academy of Apologetics in Strasbourg, France*

"*The Reason I Believe* is a fitting title for this book, because my good friend Allen Quist has been a prominent leader in explaining the reasons for being a Christian for decades as a professor and state legislator. This is a clear explanation of Christian evidential apologetics, appropriate for the college classroom and below. Professor Quist ably explains the ministerial use of reason in the Bible by going through passage after passage of Scripture in which Christ and His followers use reason to explain and defend the Christian faith. His explanation of natural law and its use in apologetics is the best I've ever seen."

—*John A. Eidsmoe, Colonel, MSSG*
Pastor, Assn. of Free Lutheran Congregations
Professor, Oak Brook College of Law & Government Policy

"In *The Reason I Believe*, Allen Quist reveals 'the forgotten and untold secret of our time' (p. 163), namely, that the apostles grounded their teaching of Christ's resurrection upon well-supported and widely known facts, which secular authorities also documented during the first and second centuries AD. Quist identifies four objective criteria by which to distinguish true from false prophets in the Old Testament era, and four objective criteria by which to distinguish reliable from unreliable accounts of the chief events recorded in the New Testament. Avoiding academic jargon, he makes Christian apologetics accessible to a broad audience, equipping the rising generation to 'share the gospel and the evidence of its truth' (p. 161)."

—*Ryan C. MacPherson, PhD*
Chair, Dept. of History,
Bethany Lutheran College, Mankato, Minnesota

"Allen Quist's book *The Reason I Believe: The Basics of Christian Apologetics* is a remarkable contribution to the defence of biblical faith. Most writers in the field restrict themselves to a very narrow, philosophical-theological approach, betraying their own lack of contact with today's world of unbelief. In diametric contrast, Professor Quist, with dual careers in college teaching and active politics, offers exactly the kind of answers so badly needed. His book is focused, literary, and solid in Reformation scholarship—just the thing for pastors and church members who want to reach the seeking unbeliever but do not know how to do it."

—*Dr. John Warwick Montgomery, PhD (Chicago),*
DThéol (Strasbourg), LLD (Cardiff)
Professor-at-Large, 1517: The Legacy Project, Irvine, CA, USA
Director, International Academy of Apologetics, Evangelism,
and Human Rights, Strasbourg, France

"The word *apologetics* scares a lot of people, because they think that refers to an exceedingly intellectual treatment of complex matters. Such is not the case with this book. Allen Quist offers us an extremely readable, biblical presentation in clear and accessible language. This book is thoroughly scriptural and impressively relevant. And Quist's occasional use of the insights of C. S. Lewis warms my heart!"

—*Dr. Joel Heck, Professor of Theology, Concordia University Texas*

THE REASON I BELIEVE

THE BASICS OF CHRISTIAN APOLOGETICS

ALLEN QUIST
Foreword by Dr. Adam Francisco

CONCORDIA PUBLISHING HOUSE • SAINT LOUIS

Published by Concordia Publishing House
3558 S. Jefferson Ave., St. Louis, MO 63118-3968
1-800-325-3040 • www.cph.org

Copyright © 2017 by Allen Quist

All rights reserved. No part of this publication may be reproduced, stored in a retrieval system, or transmitted, in any form or by any means, electronic, mechanical, photocopying, recording, or otherwise, without the prior written permission of Concordia Publishing House.

Scripture quotations are from the ESV® Bible (The Holy Bible, English Standard Version®), copyright © 2001 by Crossway, a publishing ministry of Good News Publishers. Used by permission. All rights reserved.

The quotations from the Lutheran Confessions in this publication are from *Concordia: The Lutheran Confessions*, second edition; edited by Paul McCain et al., copyright © 2006 Concordia Publishing House. All rights reserved.

Quotations marked AE in this publication are from Luther's Works, American Edition (75 vols.; St. Louis: Concordia Publishing House and Philadelphia: Muhlenberg and Fortress, 1955–).

Quotations from *What Luther Says: A Practical In-Home Anthology for the Active Christian*, compiled by Ewald M. Plass, copyright © 1959 Concordia Publishing House. All rights reserved.

Manufactured in the United States of America

Library of Congress Cataloging-in-Publication Data
    Names: Quist, Allen, author.
    Title: The reason I believe : the basics of Christian apologetics / Allen Quist ; foreword by Dr. Adam Francisco.
    Description: St. Louis : Concordia Publishing House, 2017. | Includes bibliographical references and index.
    Identifiers: LCCN 2017034619 (print) | LCCN 2017039265 (ebook) | ISBN 9780758657817 | ISBN 9780758657800 (alk. paper)
    Subjects: LCSH: Apologetics.
    Classification: LCC BT1103 (ebook) | LCC BT1103 .Q57 2017 (print) | DDC 239--dc23
    LC record available at https://lccn.loc.gov/2017034619

1 2 3 4 5 6 7 8 9 10   26 25 24 23 22 21 20 19 18 17

CONTENTS

Foreword 7

Part 1: Going Back to the Basics

    Chapter 1: What Is Christian Apologetics? 10

    Chapter 2: Peter's Use of Apologetics at Pentecost 17

Part 2: Presenting the Evidence for Christianity

    Chapter 3: Four Arguments for the Existence of God 28

    Chapter 4: God Revealed 40

    Chapter 5: Jesus, the Master Teacher and Messiah 57

    Chapter 6: Miracles 65

    Chapter 7: Fulfillment of Prophecy 74

    Chapter 8: The Resurrection and Alternate Theories 88

    Chapter 9: Eyewitness Testimony and the Validity
               of the Gospels 101

    Chapter 10: Historical Artifacts 110

    Chapter 11: Love without Limits 119

Part 3: Answering Objections

    Chapter 12: The Problem of Evil 122

    Chapter 13: The Problem of Darwinism 131

Part 4: Defending the Moral Law

    Chapter 14: Natural Law 150

Conclusion and Application 170

Answers to End-of-Chapter Questions 175

Bibliography 186

Scripture Index 191

About the Author 194

FOREWORD

Apologetics is the task of defending the Christian faith. Examples of it abound throughout the course of Church history—from the apostle Paul at Mars Hill to the 1940s BBC broadcast talks of C. S. Lewis that were eventually published as *Mere Christianity*. And, certainly, the twenty-first century has seen its fair share of apologetic activity. There are quite literally hundreds (even thousands) of books, websites, documentaries, and other media that address the various challenges of our day. But much of this material is either highly technical or focused on a specific challenge. So there is and always will be a need for a basic orientation to the apologetic task that is broad in scope but incisive in focus. *The Reason I Believe* provides exactly that.

Over the course of fourteen chapters, this book introduces its readers to the essentials of the apologetic task. After first answering the important question of "What is Christian apologetics?" and offering biblical examples of how the apostle Peter himself used apologetics, this book immediately focuses, as did Peter at Pentecost, where any proper Christian apologetic ought to begin—with a defense of the deity and, therefore, the authority of Christ. This is followed by chapter-length treatments of other essential topics such as arguments for the existence of God, the reliability of the Old Testament, a biblical response to the problem of evil, and the scientific problems with Darwinism. And to all this is added a final chapter promoting the use of natural-law reasoning in non-Christian environments.

Throughout the work, Professor Quist remains committed to a fact-based defense of Christianity. This is distinct, for a good portion of contemporary works on apologetics take a more philosophical approach. Those that do so typically go on the offense and attack non-Christian worldviews by exposing their logical inconsistencies. This is normally followed by a description of the Christian worldview by highlighting its internal coherence and consistency with the basic laws of logic and other philosophical first principles.

But our culture is philosophically illiterate. Appeals to philosophical first principles and the laws of logic are often lost on people. But it is hard to dismiss facts. They are, as John Adams famously put it, stubborn things. They stand out as evidence of something that cannot merely be written off or forgotten. They remain a firm and unalterable witness to events of the past.

Here is where Professor Quist distinguishes himself. He presents and advances fact upon fact—including some that are often overlooked—to demonstrate the correspondence between the world of hard fact and the claims of Christianity. It is this relationship that illustrates and verifies the meaningfulness and truthfulness of Christianity. No other religion or worldview can account for itself this way.

The subsequent pages of this book will be well worth your time and attention. In an age such as ours, with all its moral and religious confusion, a basic orientation to apologetics is becoming increasingly vital for all Christians, including both pastors and laity. Professor Quist has achieved just the right balance for both, providing a robust yet succinct overview of the evidence of the Christian faith.

Dr. Adam Francisco

PART 1

GOING BACK TO THE
BASICS

CHAPTER 1

WHAT IS CHRISTIAN APOLOGETICS?[1]

In 1521, Martin Luther was called before Holy Roman Emperor Charles V at the Diet of Worms (*diet* meaning "a formal meeting," and Worms being a city south of Frankfurt). At that meeting, Charles demanded that Luther recant all he had said challenging the authority of the pope and the Roman Catholic Church. What Charles heard instead was Luther's defiant statement:

> Unless I am convinced by the teachings of Holy Scriptures or by sound reasoning—for I do not believe either pope or councils alone, since they have often made mistakes and have even said the exact opposite about the same point—I am tied by the Scriptures I have quoted and by my conscience. I cannot and will not recant anything, for to go against conscience is neither safe nor right. Here I stand. God help me. Amen.[2]

With these few words, Luther clarified one of the most important principles of orthodox Christianity—that all doctrine must have its foundation solely on God's Word. This standard applies to Christian apologetics as well.

While Bible studies usually focus on matters of teaching—on doctrine, and rightly so—a study on apologetics, in contrast, does not concentrate on doctrine, at least not directly, but rather on whether the basis of our doctrine, the Bible, is trustworthy. Christian apologetics deals with the question of whether Scripture—and Christianity—is true.

The word *apologetics* comes from the Greek word ἀπολογία (*apologia*), which means "to defend a person or thing."[3] The *Anchor Bible Dictionary* defines

---

1 This chapter could also be called "What Is Lutheran Apologetics?" because it is based on the Lutheran principle that Scripture alone forms the foundation for our faith and life.
2 Nohl, *Luther*, 107.
3 Thayer, *Greek-English Lexicon*, 65.

apologetics as being "the art of persuasion employed by the Early Christians."[4] Dr. Rod Rosenbladt explained that apologetics is the presentation of arguments for the truthfulness of the Christian faith.[5]

Christian apologetics deals with the question of whether Scripture—and Christianity—is true.

The apostle Peter admonished us to be ready to make use of apologetics. In 1 Peter, he wrote that we should always be "prepared to make a defense to anyone who asks you for a reason for the hope that is in you; yet do it with gentleness and respect" (3:15).[6] That is, we should be ready to present our reasons, including our evidence, for being Christians. We derive our English term *Christian apologetics* from this text in 1 Peter.

The main application of apologetics is to mission work and evangelism. In America, up until the 1980s or so, Christians could verify the Gospel message simply by quoting the Bible. That is not always the case today—we can no longer assume that mission prospects see the Bible as trustworthy. Even many churches and church-related institutions actually deny that the Bible is reliable. Some of these bodies accordingly also deny that the Bible is God's Word. In a sense, we are back to New Testament times, when neither Jesus nor the apostles assumed their listeners would believe what they said just because they said it. Neither did the apostles assume that non-Jewish listeners would recognize the authority of the Old Testament. For these reasons, Jesus and the apostles presented evidence to demonstrate that what they said was true. Today, Christians do well to follow their example.

Additionally, the Greek word *apologia* has two parts: *apo*, meaning "from," and *logia*, as used in 1 Peter 3:15, meaning "logic."[7] Peter urged us to be ready to defend the Christian Gospel message and to do so from logic, that is, by providing arguments and evidence to substantiate the truth of the Gospel message. Here, "providing arguments and evidence" does not refer to using philosophical discourses or speculation. On the contrary, it's referring to the presentation of hard facts—the kind of evidence an attorney would use in a court of law, the kind of evidence the Bible itself used to substantiate its truthfulness: historical artifacts, credible documents, eyewitness reports, and the like.

In New Testament times, *apologia* was commonly used to denote a speech of a defendant in a court of law. In such a speech, a defendant would present

---

4 *Anchor Bible Dictionary*, 302.
5 Rosenbladt, "Beyond Culture Wars," 1.
6 This passage is usually considered to be the *sedes doctrinæ* (basis) for Christian apologetics.
7 Thayer, *Greek-English Lexicon*, 381.

reasons and evidence in an attempt to disprove the accusations against him. In 1 Peter 3, Peter implored us to be ready to give our reasons for the hope that we have. That is, we should be ready to give our reasons, including our evidence, for believing that the Gospel message of Jesus Christ is true.

In his second epistle, Peter gave us a striking example of how he personally presented such evidence. He said, "For we did not follow cleverly devised myths when we made known to you the power and coming of our Lord Jesus Christ, but we were eyewitnesses of His majesty" (2 Peter 1:16). Here, Peter argued that we can be assured of the truthfulness of everything he told us because he and other disciples were there; they were eyewitnesses of Jesus in all His divine glory. Peter meant that he and the other apostles were eyewitnesses in the same sense that someone is an eyewitness in a court of law—someone who can give trustworthy testimony because he was there and saw and heard it all for himself (see 1 Corinthians 15:5-8).

John's Gospel provides us with numerous examples of the reasons Peter said we should be ready to supply to those who are willing to hear. John, for example, explained that the reason so many people came to welcome Jesus into Jerusalem is they had heard that Jesus had raised Lazarus from the dead (John 12:18). John also explained why he recorded these reasons and evidence when he said, "Now Jesus did many other signs in the presence of the disciples, which are not written in this book; but these are written so that you may believe that Jesus is the Christ, the Son of God, and that by believing you may have life in His name" (John 20:30-31). John told us that he recorded many of the "signs" (miracles) Jesus performed so we would have evidence, so we would have proof, that Jesus is who He said He was—the promised Messiah, God in the flesh and Savior of the world. John also explained why he wanted us to conclude that Jesus is the Messiah—namely, that "by believing you may have life in His name" (v. 31). The purpose of apologetics is leading lost sinners to a saving faith in Jesus Christ. Apologetics is not about winning arguments; it's all about leading people to faith in Jesus, the Messiah.

> Apologetics is not about winning arguments; it's all about leading people to faith in Jesus, the Messiah.

In other words, the purpose of apologetics is demonstrating the truth of the glorious message that Jesus Christ, God in the flesh, came to live a perfect life and die a sinner's death in our place so that by faith in Him we can be forgiven and live in fellowship with Him in the here and now and forever in paradise.

About this Gospel message, Paul said, "For I am not ashamed of the gospel, for it is the power of God for salvation to everyone who believes, to the Jew first and also to the Greek" (Romans 1:16). Genuine, Bible-based apologetics is effective because it leads lost sinners to Christ. The power to save is not in the promotion of living of a good life, nor is it achieved by obtaining sophisticated understanding or knowledge. The power to save lost sinners is in the Gospel message of Jesus Christ and in this Gospel message alone.

> Genuine, Bible-based apologetics is effective because it leads lost sinners to Christ.

When Paul said the Gospel is the "power of God for salvation to everyone who believes" (v. 16), he was speaking of much more than just an intellectual assent on our part as to something being true. He was referring to receiving a new spiritual life of faith that is accomplished only by the power of the Holy Spirit. This new spiritual life is God's gift to us because of His grace and His grace alone. Only God can create this new spiritual life of faith, as Paul said, "For by grace you have been saved through faith. And this is not your own doing; it is the gift of God, not a result of works, so that no one may boast" (Ephesians 2:8–9).

In His conversation with Nicodemus, Jesus Himself emphasized that faith is a new spiritual life created by the Holy Spirit. Jesus said,

> "Truly, truly, I say to you, unless one is born again, he cannot see the kingdom of God." Nicodemus said to Him, "How can a man be born when he is old? Can he enter a second time into his mother's womb and be born?" Jesus answered, "Truly, truly, I say to you, unless one is born of water and the Spirit, he cannot enter the kingdom of God. That which is born of the flesh is flesh, and that which is born of the Spirit is spirit." (John 3:3–8)

In this way, Jesus clarified that saving faith is far more than a mental conclusion we come to in our own minds. Here, Jesus explained that the creation of saving faith is a miracle, a creative act of God the Holy Spirit. By creating faith in us, the Holy Spirit has called into existence something that wasn't there before—a new living spiritual entity that is now part of who we are and unites us in fellowship with God Himself. The role of apologetics is to help us realize that this glorious Gospel message is true, and when we heed this message, the Holy Spirit creates a living faith within us.

TWO FORMS OF APOLOGETICS

There are two forms of apologetics: *offensive* and *defensive*. The apostle John illustrated offensive apologetics in his explanation of why he recorded many of the signs Jesus performed, especially the resurrection (John 20:30–31). John did so, he said, to convince his readers that Jesus truly is the long-awaited Messiah. Offensive apologetics directly points to the truth of the Gospel message. Jesus gave us numerous examples of this type of apologetics—for example, when He raised Lazarus from the dead (John 11:38–44). Even Jesus' enemies recognized the significance of evidence like this, saying, "'If we let Him go on like this, everyone will believe in Him'" (v. 48).

Defensive apologetics, in contrast, consists of answering objections to Christianity. Defensive apologetics is like driving a car on icy roads in winter—we know where we wish to go, but sometimes we must overcome some serious obstacles to get there. Jesus made use of defensive apologetics in the following debate between Himself and the Jewish Pharisees:

> Then a demon-oppressed man who was blind and mute was brought to Him, and He healed him, so that the man spoke and saw. And all the people were amazed, and said, "Can this be the Son of David?" But when the Pharisees heard it, they said, "It is only by Beelzebul, the prince of demons, that this man casts out demons." Knowing their thoughts, He said to them, "Every kingdom divided against itself is laid waste, and no city or house divided against itself will stand. And if Satan casts out Satan, he is divided against himself. How then will his kingdom stand? And if I cast out demons by Beelzebul, by whom do your sons cast them out? Therefore they will be your judges. But if it is by the Spirit of God that I cast out demons, then the kingdom of God has come upon you. Or how can someone enter a strong man's house and plunder his goods, unless he first binds the strong man? Then indeed he may plunder his house." (Matthew 12:22–29)

Here, the Pharisees were alleging that Jesus performed miracles by Satan's power, not God's. Jesus refuted this accusation by explaining their objection was irrational because Satan would not weaken his own kingdom by casting out demons. By answering the Pharisees' objection, Jesus also told His listeners that the only reasonable explanation for His miracles was that He did them by the power of God, meaning He was speaking by God's authority and was, therefore, speaking the truth. Jesus' use of defensive apologetics began by refuting the objection of the Pharisees. Then, by means of sound logic, He proceeded to a powerful proclamation that the Messiah had come and now stood before them. All Christian apologetics, either directly or indirectly, points to the message that Jesus is the Messiah of God, who came to save lost sinners.

Why, then, did most of the Pharisees reject Him? Jesus answered that question when He said: "'And this is the judgment: the light has come into the world, and people loved the darkness rather than the light because their works were evil. For everyone who does wicked things hates the light and does not come to the light, lest his works should be exposed'" (John 3:19–20). Jesus also said to the Jewish people, "How often would I have gathered your children together as a hen gathers her brood under her wings, and you were not willing!" (Luke 13:34). People don't reject Christianity for lack of evidence; they do so because they refuse to believe. As Jesus said in Luke 16:31, "If they do not hear Moses and the Prophets, neither will they be convinced if someone should rise from the dead." History demonstrated the truth of Jesus' words when the Pharisees and skeptics refused to believe even when Jesus Himself rose from the dead.

> People don't reject Christianity for lack of evidence; they do so because they refuse to believe.

In closing this chapter, we recognize that the principles we have considered present us with a bit of a paradox: since being a Christian is totally a matter of faith in Jesus and entirely the result of God's grace operating by the power of the Holy Spirit through the Word and Sacraments (Baptism and the Lord's Supper), how, then, can evidence have anything to do with it? In answer, we see that the evidence for the truth of Christianity is part and parcel of the Word's testimony to the Gospel of Christ. Jesus' miracles, His fulfillment of messianic prophecy, His resurrection, and His establishment of eyewitness accounts are all essential components of the Word's testimony to the saving Gospel message. The doctrine of God's declaration that we are forgiven and are, therefore, righteous because of what Christ has done for us—and the evidence for its truth—are both essential parts of the Gospel message. The doctrine and its verification are intertwined.[8]

By itself, however, defensive apologetics gets us nowhere. In evangelism and mission work, Christians use defensive apologetics to make offensive apologetics possible. Defensive apologetics is useful for removing barriers to the Christian faith. We use it to create openings for the successful proclamation of Jesus, the Savior of the world, just as Jesus Himself used it in the example above from Matthew 12. The power of God to save sinners is in the Gospel and only in the Gospel. Apologetics is sort of like a football game—we sometimes need to play defense in order to get the ball back and move it in the right direction while on offense. Our goal with apologetics, always, is effectively presenting the saving message of Jesus Christ to all who are lost.

---

8 Christian apologetics makes use of the ministerial use of reason—that is, reason as an instrument based on God's Word—but Christian apologetics rejects the magisterial use of reason, reason that places itself above God's Word. Christian apologetics rejects rationalism as a methodology for knowing religious truth.

QUESTIONS FOR REVIEW AND DISCUSSION
1. What if a non-Christian were to ask you why he or she should become a Christian instead of a follower of another religion? What would you say?
2. How do you think the apostle John might have answered that question?

(The rest of this book is intended to provide additional information that should be helpful in answering questions such as these.)

CHAPTER 2

PETER'S USE OF APOLOGETICS AT PENTECOST

This chapter further explains the nature of Christian apologetics by describing how Jesus' twelve disciples—in particular, the apostle Peter—used apologetics in their proclamation of the Christian Gospel message. The disciples were committed to telling the world only what was true and would give the world the best possible evidence to demonstrate that the Gospel message was true. We will focus on the apologetic content of the first recorded speech (also known as a sermon) given by one of Jesus' disciples, Peter, whose speech to the onlookers on the day of Pentecost is recorded in Acts 2.

ACTS 2:1: PETER EXPLAINS IMPORTANT CRITERIA FOR BEING ONE OF THE TWELVE

Acts 2 begins as follows: "When the day of Pentecost arrived, they were all together in one place" (v. 1).

To understand the apologetic nature of Peter's sermon, we first need to understand who Luke, the author of Acts, was describing when he said "they." Who were these people who were filled with the Holy Spirit on Pentecost? For this answer, we look to the first chapter of Acts, where Peter clarified that on the day of Pentecost there were only eleven disciples present because Judas had committed suicide (Acts 1:18–19).

Peter then described the necessary qualifications for any man to be eligible to replace Judas. He said:

> "So one of the men who have accompanied us during all the time that the Lord Jesus went in and out among us, beginning from the baptism of John until the day when he was taken up from us—one of these men must become with us a witness to His resurrection." (Acts 1:21–22)

Peter, here, emphasized that for anyone to be an acceptable replacement for Judas, he must have been with Jesus for the entirety of Jesus' earthly ministry, including His Baptism, death, resurrection, and ascension into heaven. He further clarified that to be part of Jesus' inner circle of disciples, the man must have personally witnessed everything so he could serve as a witness to the world regarding everything Jesus had said and done.

To understand the significance of this criterion, we must recognize that by the word *witness*, Peter meant *eyewitness*. Peter was referring to the kind of witness who, for instance, would be of particular importance in a court of law—someone who could give reliable, firsthand information about what Jesus had said and done. Peter made it clear that someone possessing secondhand accounts or unsubstantiated stories would not be allowed. He and the other disciples made sure they would give the public only that testimony which was completely accurate. That way, the public would have good reason to recognize it as such. The disciples subsequently chose a man named Matthias to replace Judas.

ACTS 2:2-15: PETER REFUTES FALSE ACCUSATIONS

Acts 2 continues as follows:

> And suddenly there came from heaven a sound like a mighty rushing wind, and it filled the entire house where they were sitting. And divided tongues as of fire appeared to them and rested on each one of them. And they were all filled with the Holy Spirit and began to speak in other tongues as the Spirit gave them utterance.
>
> Now there were dwelling in Jerusalem Jews, devout men from every nation under heaven. And at this sound the multitude came together, and they were bewildered, because each one was hearing them speak in his own language. And they were amazed and astonished, saying, "Are not all these who are speaking Galileans? And how is it that we hear, each of us in his own native language? Parthians and Medes and Elamites and residents of Mesopotamia, Judea and Cappadocia, Pontus and Asia, Phrygia and Pamphylia, Egypt and the parts of Libya belonging to Cyrene, and visitors from Rome, both Jews and proselytes, Cretans and Arabians—we hear them telling in our own tongues the mighty works of God." And all were amazed and perplexed, saying to one another, "What does this mean?" But others mocking said, "They are filled with new wine."

But Peter, standing with the eleven, lifted up his voice and addressed them: "Men of Judea and all who dwell in Jerusalem, let this be known to you, and give ear to my words. For these people are not drunk, as you suppose, since it is only the third hour of the day. (vv. 2–15)

Peter continued his sermon by refuting the false accusation that he and the other apostles were speaking in the native languages of their listeners because they were drunk. To refute this allegation, Peter appealed to the common knowledge of his Jewish audience, who knew that at that time Jews did not drink to excess in the early morning hours. (It's not that they never drank too much, but if they did so, it was in the evening, not in the morning.) By example, Peter shows us that there are times when we, too, should answer objections to the Gospel message since these objections may prevent our audience from hearing the message of Christ.

ACTS 2:16–21: PETER DELIVERS HIS FIRST ARGUMENT

Peter continued by saying:

But this is what was uttered through the prophet Joel:

"'And in the last days it shall be, God declares,
that I will pour out my Spirit on all flesh,
and your sons and your daughters shall prophesy,
and your young men shall see visions,
and your old men shall dream dreams;
even on My male servants and female servants
in those days I will pour out My Spirit, and they shall prophesy.
And I will show wonders in the heavens above
and signs on the earth below,
blood, and fire, and vapor of smoke;
the sun shall be turned to darkness
and the moon to blood,
before the day of the Lord comes, the great and magnificent day.
And it shall come to pass that everyone who calls upon the name of the Lord shall be saved.'" (2:16–21)

Peter here presents his first line of argument and evidence for the truth of the Gospel message—namely, that his audience was witnessing the partial fulfillment of the Old Testament prediction of the prophet Joel that the coming of the Messiah would be accompanied by miraculous events, including the outpouring of the Holy Spirit on both men and women, young and old, and even on those of lowly estate.[9] In this way, Peter began to develop his first argument for the truth of the message of Jesus as Savior of the world—that Jesus fulfilled the messianic prophecies of the Old Testament.

ACTS 2:22-23: PETER DELIVERS HIS SECOND ARGUMENT

Peter then said: "Men of Israel, hear these words: Jesus of Nazareth, a man attested to you by God with mighty works and wonders and signs that God did through Him in your midst, as you yourselves know" (2:22).

This is Peter's second argument for the truth of his message—that Jesus performed numerous and sensational miracles in their midst and thereby established the His own authenticity and the truthfulness of His claims. As proof, Peter again appealed to what was commonly known among the Jews; he said, "You yourselves know [of these miracles]" (v. 22). The miracles of Jesus were, in fact, widely recognized, and as we will see later, even Jesus' enemies admitted He performed miracles.

Since Peter was speaking to a Jewish audience, they would have known that one of the characteristics of true prophets of God was their ability to perform miracles. Up until the time of Jesus, no prophet had met this test more admirably than Moses, who was instrumental in the parting of the Red Sea—a sensational miracle that allowed the Israelites to cross over the sea on dry ground while the pursuing Egyptian army was drowned (Exodus 14:13-31). Even the Samaritan woman with whom Jesus spoke at the well of Sychar understood this test—the ability to perform miracles—for determining true prophets. When Jesus revealed to her that He knew things no ordinary man would have known, the woman at the well replied by saying, "Sir, I perceive that You are a prophet" (John 4:19).

We should notice that Peter appealed to nonbiblical evidence to establish his assertion that Jesus performed miracles when he said, "As you yourselves know" (Acts 2:22). Peter understood his audience, knowing they would have received numerous reports—nonbiblical reports—about the miracles of Jesus. We previously observed that Peter also used nonbiblical information to answer the objection about drunkenness. Peter's example indicates that we, too, should not only understand to whom we are speaking but also make use of nonbiblical information in our evangelism and mission work. This nonbiblical information includes secular historical records as well as the records

---

9   As is not unusual for messianic prophecies, Joel described signs of both the first and the second comings of the Messiah.

of those associated with the New Testament Church. It also includes historical artifacts that verify the biblical records as well as provide additional details to the what the Bible records. (We will discuss more of this in the following chapters.)

We should also note that Peter forcefully proclaimed that his listeners had broken God's moral law by saying, "This Jesus, delivered up according to the definite plan and foreknowledge of God, you crucified and killed by the hands of lawless men" (2:23). Peter's sermon, and every sermon recorded in Acts, contains both Law and Gospel. There are no exceptions.

Peter's sermon, and every sermon recorded in Acts, contains both Law and Gospel. There are no exceptions.

ACTS 2:24–32: PETER DELIVERS HIS THIRD ARGUMENT

Peter then said:

"God raised Him up, loosing the pangs of death, because it was not possible for Him to be held by it. For David says concerning Him,

'I saw the Lord always before me,
    for He is at my right hand that I may not be shaken;
therefore my heart was glad, and my tongue rejoiced;
    my flesh also will dwell in hope.
For You will not abandon my soul to Hades,
    or let Your Holy One see corruption.
You have made known to me the paths of life;
    You will make me full of gladness with Your presence.'

"Brothers, I may say to you with confidence about the patriarch David that he both died and was buried, and his tomb is with us to this day. Being therefore a prophet, and knowing that God had sworn with an oath to him that He would set one of his descendants on his throne, he foresaw and spoke about the resurrection of the Christ, that He was not abandoned to Hades, nor did His flesh see corruption. This Jesus God raised up, and of that we all are witnesses." (vv. 24–32)

This brings us to the third and most important piece of evidence Peter presented in support of Jesus being the Messiah of God: His resurrection from the dead. We notice the fulfillment of prophecy and the testimony of numerous eyewitnesses are used to verify the truth of Jesus' resurrection. The arguments for the truthfulness of the Gospel message are intertwined.

> **In the resurrection, doctrine and apologetics are interconnected.**

We also notice that the resurrection of Jesus is far more than apologetics—it is also a critical doctrine of Christian theology. In the resurrection, doctrine and apologetics are interconnected.

Jesus Himself had predicted that the primary evidence for His being the Messiah would be His resurrection from the dead:

> So the Jews said to Him, "What sign do you show us for doing these things?" Jesus answered them, "Destroy this temple, and in three days I will raise it up." The Jews then said, "It has taken forty-six years to build this temple, and will You raise it up in three days?" But He was speaking about the temple of His body. When therefore He was raised from the dead, His disciples remembered that He had said this, and they believed the Scripture and the word that Jesus had spoken. (John 2:18–22)

It would be difficult to overstate the profound impact Jesus' resurrection had on His disciples. The effect of the resurrection on Thomas is recorded for us in John's Gospel:

> Eight days later, His disciples were inside again, and Thomas was with them. Although the doors were locked, Jesus came and stood among them and said, "Peace be with you." Then He said to Thomas, "Put your finger here, and see My hands; and put out your hand, and place it in My side. Do not disbelieve, but believe." Thomas answered him, "My Lord and my God!" (20:26–28)

The response of the other disciples must have been similar. Something incredible must have happened on that Easter Sunday to transform disciples who were once frightened, disillusioned, confused, and directionless men into courageous and highly focused spokesmen for the marvelous good news that Jesus had risen from the dead. As a consequence of Jesus' resurrection, they insisted and knew beyond all doubt that He was indeed the Messiah of God, who had come to seek and to save those who are lost.

This radical change in the disciples was not what anyone had expected. The Jewish rulers had bribed the Roman guards to say the disciples had stolen Jesus' body. So if the resurrection was a lie, these disciples knew it was a lie. But all the disciples were willing to die, several of them by crucifixion, rather than change their story. And while people may die for a lie, they won't die for something they *know* is a lie. The disciples were so bold because they knew beyond all doubt Jesus had risen; they had seen Him with their own eyes. And because of His resurrection, they knew that they, too, would rise from the dead just as Jesus had!

ACTS 2:32: PETER DELIVERS HIS FOURTH ARGUMENT

Peter then utilized his fourth argument as proof for the truth of his claim that Jesus was the Messiah of God when he said, "This Jesus God raised up, and of that we all are witnesses."

We have already spoken of the importance of eyewitness testimony to the truth of the Christian message. Here, Peter specifically included this evidence in his Pentecost speech as his fourth line of argument. The Early New Testament Church, as well as the apostles, relied on the criterion of eyewitness testimony not only to determine who was a trustworthy authority on what Jesus had said and done but also to identify which writings were reliable and authoritative and which were not. As a consequence, we know the books we have in our New Testament were accepted as authoritative because they were written by, or based on the accounts of, eyewitnesses.[10] The second-century and later apocryphal gospels,[11] in contrast, were never accepted by the Church because they did not contain, nor were they based on, eyewitness accounts. Books and movies such as *The Da Vinci Code* may have given these second-century writings an aura of credibility, but it's an aura they do not deserve. It's important to remember that in some cases we are dealing with *fiction*—not history.

ACTS 2:33-41: PETER CONCLUDES WITH ADDITIONAL EVIDENCE

Peter then concluded his speech by saying this:

> "Being therefore exalted at the right hand of God, and having received from the Father the promise of the Holy Spirit, He has poured out this that you yourselves are seeing and hearing. For David did not ascend into the heavens, but he himself says,
>
>> "'The Lord said to My Lord,
>> "Sit at My right hand,

---

[10] Tertullian (AD 160–225) stressed the criterion of apostolicity as the primary test for a writing being authoritative. He also distinguished between Gospels of apostolic origin such as Matthew and John and Gospels written by disciples of apostles, those being Mark and Luke. He viewed both as authoritative. See Tertullian, *Against Marcion*, book 4, par. 5, *Ante-Nicene Fathers*, vol. 1, 350.

[11] The *apocryphal* gospels were accounts of the life of Jesus that were neither written by, nor based upon, the eyewitnesses of the events described. For that reason, they were never accepted by the New Testament Church as authoritative or as part of the canon.

until I make Your enemies Your footstool."'

Let all the house of Israel therefore know for certain that God has made Him both Lord and Christ, this Jesus whom you crucified."

Now when they heard this they were cut to the heart, and said to Peter and the rest of the apostles, "Brothers, what shall we do?" And Peter said to them, "Repent and be baptized every one of you in the name of Jesus Christ for the forgiveness of your sins, and you will receive the gift of the Holy Spirit. For the promise is for you and for your children and for all who are far off, everyone whom the Lord our God calls to Himself." And with many other words he bore witness and continued to exhort them, saying, "Save yourselves from this crooked generation." So those who received his word were baptized, and there were added that day about three thousand souls. (vv. 33–41)

Peter ended his sermon by adding more evidence to the arguments he had already presented. He then emphasized the Gospel by calling on his listeners to "repent and be baptized . . . for the forgiveness of your sins" and by saying, "For the promise is for you and your children and for all who are far off, everyone whom the Lord our God calls to Himself" (vv. 38–39).

Looking at Peter's Pentecost sermon overall, we should ask ourselves: Did Peter speak like a teacher, explaining important information? Or did he speak more like an attorney in a court of law, providing arguments and evidence to persuade his listeners to accept the truthfulness of his claims? Clearly, Peter spoke more like an attorney, more like a debater, than a teacher. Peter's methodology was to explain the Christian message and then provide evidence to back up what he said. His procedure was to make claims of truth, provide evidence, make another claim of truth, and provide more evidence. Truth followed by evidence is the methodology of a debater—and the methodology of the Christian apologist.

> Truth followed by evidence is the methodology of a debater—and the methodology of the Christian apologist.

Every sermon recorded in Acts is similar to Peter's Pentecost speech. For that reason, we need to ask ourselves if we are doing evangelism and mission work the same way today. Are we answering the objections to the Gospel that stand in the way of our audience being able to hear the message? Are we providing proof for the truthfulness of the message we are proclaiming?

Can we assume our listeners regard the Bible as reliable?

Do they even believe God exists, or do they think the reality of evil rules out the existence of a loving and all-powerful God? Do our listeners recognize the existence of right and wrong? Or do they think morality is merely what's right and wrong in their own eyes?

The world today is far different from what it was one or two generations ago, and so our testimony to this world needs to be different too. In many ways, we are back to the first century where the evangelists had to start virtually from square one. On Mars Hill, Paul began with the common ground of recognition of an unknown god (Acts 17:22–31). Today, we may need to become even more basic than that. For some individuals, we might have to begin with reasons for believing that there is a God, as we will consider in the next chapter. It is not unusual for converts to Christianity to first conclude that God exists, or at least may exist, as was the case with C. S. Lewis, before they can take the Gospel message seriously. We will frequently need to provide reasons as to why the Bible is trustworthy as well. There are many today who believe the Bible is full of errors and was written by people other than those whose names are attached to particular books. Chapter 9 will provide information on the reliability of the Bible.

New Testament evangelism and mission work called for far more than a simple explanation. It called for evidence to prove that the message of Christ was true. We are in the same position today. Realizing this is so, we do well to model our testimony after the example of the New Testament apostles. As we have seen, they used four overall lines of evidence. They are as follows:

1. Jesus and the apostles verified the truthfulness of their claims by performing many sensational miracles.
2. We know that Jesus is the Messiah of God because He fulfilled the messianic prophecies of the Old Testament.
3. Jesus provided extraordinary proof for His claim to be the Messiah by rising from the dead.
4. We know that the New Testament documents are reliable because they were written by, or based on, the accounts of those who were eyewitnesses of what Jesus had said and done. These eyewitnesses were persecuted and most were killed for their faith.

These arguments are primarily based on information recorded for us in Scripture. As we have also noted, however, the apostles commonly employed nonbiblical evidence in support of these assertions as well. And because we are now two thousand years removed from the New Testament Church, our apologetics will in some ways be the same and in other ways be quite different from that of the apostles. We will want to use the same four lines of argument and evidence, but we additionally have a wealth of new information at our disposal. The following chapters will bring in much of this new information and also provide suggestions on how to answer today's most pressing objections to the Christian faith.

QUESTIONS FOR REVIEW AND DISCUSSION
1. Why might a pastor be more likely to include apologetics in a sermon given at a funeral than at a regular church service?
2. Christians are sometimes told, "The only reason you are a Christian is because your parents were Christian. If you had been raised a Muslim, you would be one too." How might you respond to this accusation?

PART 2

PRESENTING THE
EVIDENCE
FOR CHRISTIANITY

CHAPTER 3

FOUR ARGUMENTS FOR THE EXISTENCE OF GOD

Philosophers and theologians have pondered various arguments for the existence of God for thousands of years. Records of such deliberations go back at least as far as Socrates (469–399 BC), and these arguments, both for and against the existence of God, continue to be of significant interest today. Several of the arguments are relatively new; others have fascinating new features because of recently discovered information resulting from scientific research. In my view, there are four such arguments that are especially meaningful: (1) the argument from design, (2) the moral argument, (3) the cosmological argument, and (4) the genetic entropy argument. (While this book focuses primarily on scientific and historical evidence, this chapter is an exception in that it emphasizes philosophical considerations as well as scientific discoveries.)

These four arguments are at least partially responsible for the fact that most people throughout the world recognize the existence of a god or gods of some kind. Christians line up with the majority on this matter, of course. For example, a 2016 Gallup Poll asked Americans, "Do you believe in God?" The result was that 89 percent said yes.[12] This does not mean, however, that 89 percent of Americans believe in the triune God. Some of them are pantheists (nature is God), some are Muslims, some are Jehovah's Witnesses, and others subscribe to a variety of other non-Christian religions. This does mean that Christian evangelism can rely on the belief in a god of some kind as a common-ground starting point for most people.

We are speaking here of what is called *general revelation*, defined as God having manifested Himself through nature. The interpretation of this revelation is called *natural theology*, which refers to what we can know about God by

---

12 Newport, "Most Americans."

studying nature and drawing logical conclusions from it. General revelation is limited in that it does not explain that God is triune; nor does it convey many other truths that can only be known through *special revelation*: God having made Himself known in miraculous ways, primarily through Scripture. As 2 Timothy 3:15 states: "From childhood you have been acquainted with the sacred writings, which are able to make you wise for salvation through faith in Christ Jesus." In contrast to general revelation, special revelation focuses on God incarnate, on the God-man, Jesus Christ. The Gospel message of Christ can be known only through special revelation.

Going back to general revelation and natural theology, the apostle Paul explained that God's existence and attributes are evident from observing the world He created. Paul said:

> For what can be known about God is plain to them, because God has shown it to them. For His invisible attributes, namely, His eternal power and divine nature, have been clearly perceived, ever since the creation of the world, in the things that have been made. (Romans 1:19–20)

We draw conclusions about God and His attributes by studying nature. Just as science draws its conclusions from observations of nature, so also we conclude that God exists based on observations of nature. Science and natural theology overlap, as we will see in the following arguments. We must recognize, however, that scientific study cannot answer the biggest questions of our existence.

When well-known atheist-turned-agnostic Richard Dawkins was asked how life began, he replied by saying that he had no idea.[13] Similarly, John Horgan, writing in *Scientific American*, said that geologists, chemists, astronomers, and biologists still see the origin of life as a complete mystery.[14] And Nobel Prize–winning scientist Sir John Eccles said that from the perspective of science, we not only have no idea how life began, we have no idea how life even could have begun.[15] The existence of God, however, does provide an explanation for the origin of life and the origin of the universe. We now turn to several of the ways we can conclude from nature that God exists.

---

13 Stein, *Expelled*.
14 Horgan, "Don't tell the creationists," 118.
15 Sir John Eccles, comments made at the Gustavus Adolphus College Nobel Symposium in 1968 while I was in attendance.

THE ARGUMENT FROM DESIGN

Also called the *teleological argument*, the argument from design for the existence of God is an argument that is said to go back as far as the Greek philosopher Socrates. However, King David (1040–970 BC), articulated the argument from design much earlier. David wrote:

> The heavens declare the glory of God,
> and the sky above proclaims His handiwork.
> Day to day pours out speech,
> and night to night reveals knowledge.
> There is no speech, nor are there words,
> whose voice is not heard.
> Their voice goes out through all the earth,
> and their words to the end of the world. (Psalm 19:1–4)

Here, David explained that the magnificence of the universe proclaims the existence of a majestic Creator God. The universe has a grand design; this must mean there is a designer, an architect, behind it. The argument from design observes that many features of the universe as well as features of living things are so complex and so unique that they must be the work of an intelligent and creative mind. It is unimaginable that these features could have developed gradually and by chance. Prominent biochemist Michael Behe calls this phenomenon *irreducible complexity*. Features of living things that are irreducibly complex could not have developed gradually over time, says Behe.[16] Such features would have had to appear fully formed to have survival value. One such feature of living things is the feather.

> The argument from design observes that many features of the universe as well as features of living things are so complex and so unique that they must be the work of an intelligent and creative mind.

The origin of birds has always been a major problem for Darwinism, and even today Darwinists have no credible explanation for the origin of birds or their feathers. Feathers are highly complex and intricately designed structures that are necessary for birds to fly. Contrary to what evolutionists sometimes say, the fossil record reveals no evidence of feather evolution. There are no clearly identified transitional species.

Feathers are intricate in structure and are extremely light in weight. At the same time, they are beautifully designed and have amazing diversity in size, shape, color, and texture. Not

---

16   Behe, "Irreducible Complexity," 2.

surprisingly, they have been used by people of numerous cultures throughout history to decorate themselves in various ways.

A swan has twenty-five thousand feathers, and small birds such as wrens have more than one thousand. Most birds lose their feathers every year, a process called molting that occurs gradually so no bare spots develop. The feathers are lost and replaced in pairs, one from each side, so the bird's balance is maintained. A feather has a shaft that forms its center. On the shafts are vanes made of small strands called barbs. Each barb has thousands of smaller strands attached to it. These are called barbules. The barbules are connected to barbicels with microscopic hooklike devices called hamuli. Each strand is hooked to an opposing strand, just like the hooks on a zipper. (In fact, the invention of the zipper was the result of studying feathers.)[17]

So how could feathers possibly have developed by chance? And how could they have developed gradually? A partially formed feather would have no survival value whatsoever. One feather, even fully formed, would have no survival value. Partially formed feathers would have negative survival value. What are the chances that a random mutation could occur that would clothe a reptile with more than one thousand fully formed feathers arranged in such a way so the reptile could fly? None whatsoever.

CANADA GOOSE IN FLIGHT.
Goose flying © RC Keller / iStockphoto.com.

Canada geese, like swans, have twenty-five thousand feathers, some consisting of one million component parts. Is this really accidental? Or is it more likely to be the work of a grand designer?

Charles Darwin recognized the difficulty in explaining feathers; he also recognized the difficulty in explaining the human eye, as well as numerous other features of organisms that appear to be impossible to explain by chance and by gradual changes. Such features include the existence of flagellum (a long, lash-like appendage serving as an organ of locomotion in protozoa and

---

17   Yahya, "The Irreducible Complexity of Wings Refutes Evolution."

sperm cells) and the human ear, which equips us to hear sounds and enables us to detect the location from which those sounds are coming. Darwin additionally recognized that fossil records have failed to provide transitional fossils for such features. His proposed solution to the problem? He assured that further research would discover the needed transitional fossils. Have these missing-link fossils been discovered? They have not.

There are many other examples of living things that are amazingly complex and appear to have been incapable of arising by chance through gradual changes. Even one single cell, as in a single-cell organism, is now known to be extraordinarily complicated. Similarly, we marvel at the complexity of the DNA molecule, and yet DNA and RNA only store and transmit information. It is the information itself that is the most amazing. It is said that the information contained in the DNA of one cell of one person could not be contained in all the books in a large library. Every cell in our body contains all the information necessary to construct a living human being. And despite all the knowledge we now have, the information in our DNA may well surpass everything we know. All of this suggests the existence of a grand architect who has knowledge far superior to anything we can imagine. We call that grand architect God.

THE MORAL ARGUMENT

The moral argument for the existence of God begins with the general recognition of the existence of a universal moral code, a moral code known as natural law, also called the law of nature. (Chapter 14 describes natural law in greater detail.) The apostle Paul makes reference to this universal moral code in Romans 2:

> For when Gentiles, who do not have the law, by nature do what the law requires, they are a law to themselves, even though they do not have the law. They show that the work of the law is written on their hearts, while their conscience also bears witness, and their conflicting thoughts accuse or even excuse them. (vv. 14–15)

The United States Declaration of Independence also recognizes natural law, and it appeals to natural law as the basis for the United States' sovereignty and for basic human rights. The Declaration states:

> When in the Course of human events, it becomes necessary for one people to dissolve the political bands which have connected them with another, and to assume among the powers of the earth, the separate and equal station to which the Laws of Nature

and of Nature's God entitle them, a decent respect to the opinions of mankind requires that they should declare the causes which impel them to the separation.[18] (Emphasis added)

Not many Americans realize that our forefathers' decision to make the United States of America an independent country was based on natural law. This is an important truth our history books rarely teach, but it is not possible to understand the intended nature of government in the United States without recognizing its foundation in natural law.

Not everyone agrees that natural law is real, of course. Well-known atheist-turned-agnostic Richard Dawkins denied the existence of this universal moral code when he said that the universe we observe has no design, no purpose, no evil, and no good; it has nothing but indifference.[19]

Dawkins's rejection of the universal moral code, however, is simply a necessary consequence of his worldview. Nevertheless, even he can't function in the real world without appealing to natural law. In response to the January 7, 2015, Islamic terrorist attack in Paris, France, that killed twelve people, Richard Dawkins criticized Islam for being a religion that promotes violence.[20] But on what grounds can Dawkins object to violence? He can do so only by assuming the existence of a universal moral code that identifies violence and murder as evil and that asserts that Islamic terrorists are subject to the same moral code as are all other people. So even Dawkins himself can't live in this world without appealing to the universal moral code, a code he claims doesn't exist.

That said, the moral argument for the existence of God asserts that because there is a universal moral law, then there must also be a Lawgiver. A universal moral law cannot exist in a world without God. This argument was first known to have been formulated by German philosopher Immanuel Kant (1734–1804), but it was developed and popularized by C. S. Lewis (1898–1963).

The moral argument asserts that if the world consists of nature plus nothing (materialism), then the world can have no moral component. Guilt becomes "guilt feelings," and even items such as love and admiration disappear and are reduced to something far less—"feelings of affection." Important realities such as freedom and creativity become mere illusions. There is no morality in a test tube nor in the physics labora-

> The moral argument for the existence of God asserts that because there is a universal moral law, then there must also be a Lawgiver.

---
18   Declaration of Independence.
19   Dawkins, "Science and God," 892.
20   Dawkins, Twitter.

tory in that natural science deals with what is but cannot probe what should or should not be. There is no morality in the animal world. We may or may not like what lions do, or what wolves do, or what mosquitoes do, but we don't identify any of their actions as immoral. Why not? The reason is that only persons are governed by morality; nature is not. Writer and philosopher Fyodor Dostoevsky said that if there is no God, then everything is permitted, everything is lawful. There are then no moral rules that we are obligated to obey.[21] Just as there can be no laws in a country without a governing body that made them, so also there can be no genuine laws of right and wrong without a governing Supreme Being who made them.

As soon as we have a Creator God, however, and we additionally have creatures made in His image, then morality becomes a necessary part of the picture. A Creator God will have expectations for those creatures He has made to be like Him. If this Creator God is good, then His expectation for those He made to be like Him is that they be good also. And when we realize what these expectations are, we quickly conclude that we haven't lived up to them. C. S. Lewis described our predicament this way:

> It is after you have realized that there is a real Moral Law, and a Power behind the law, and that you have broken that law and put yourself wrong with that Power—it is after all this, and not a moment sooner, that Christianity begins to talk. When you know you are sick, you will listen to the doctor. When you have realized that our position is nearly desperate you will begin to understand what Christians are talking about.[22]

Lewis also explained that at one time he believed the existence of evil in our world ruled out the existence of a loving God. He thought that way, he said, until he realized that to recognize the existence of genuine evil assumed that God must exist too. Neither evil nor good can exist without God. So Lewis came to see that he was actually assuming God's existence in trying to disprove Him. (More on the problem of evil in chapter 12.) That realization led Lewis to admit that God exists, and since He exists, then we are accountable to Him. The answer to the desperate position this puts us in, said Lewis, is faith in the Savior God who paid the penalty for our wrongs by His death on the cross.[23] We can see, then, the logical progression that takes place. We

---

21 Dostoevsky, *Brothers Karamazov*, 200. See also chapter 14 on natural law.
22 Lewis, *Mere Christianity*, 38–39. Copyright © C. S. Lewis Pte. Ltd. 1942, 1943, 1944, 1952. Extract reprinted by permission.
23 Lewis, *Mere Christianity*, 38–39.

recognize from observing the world that genuine morality does exist. If the moral law exists, then a Lawgiver (God) must exist—a Lawgiver to whom we are accountable. When we honestly compare ourselves to the moral law, we quickly see that we haven't conformed to its demands, nor to the expectations of the Lawgiver. This realization leads us to recognize our need for a Savior.

THE COSMOLOGICAL ARGUMENT

We can easily observe that the world is in motion. The earth is in motion. All the other planets are in motion. The air moves; the oceans move; the particles in atoms are in motion, as are all forms of energy. Some force must have caused all this motion. The cosmological argument for the existence of God holds that this force, this prime mover, is God. The cosmological argument—also known as the "first cause" argument—also observes that life is one form of motion. Life only comes from other life. The ultimate source of life on earth is God.

The cosmological argument is consistent with the Book of Genesis, which says, "In the beginning, God created the heavens and the earth" (1:1). According to Genesis, the physical world and life in all its forms was created by God. And it must be recognized that Genesis is written as history—not mythology. (We will explore more about this in the next chapter.) It is written as the genuine historical account of how the universe and life on this earth came into being. God is the force behind all the motion, including the life that we observe.

> The cosmological argument for the existence of God holds that this force, this prime mover, is God.

Many people today believe that the universe is the result of a big bang, an extraordinary explosion that created all the matter and energy we perceive in the universe. As evidence of this theory, it is said that we live in an expanding universe that points to its origin in the big bang. This may all be so, but it really doesn't explain very much. Where did the matter and energy that produced the big bang come from? And why did it explode? The cosmological argument contends that there must be some first cause, or ultimate cause, for all this matter and energy; the first cause is God.

THE GENETIC ENTROPY[24] ARGUMENT

Charles Darwin and others of his time knew very little about genetics. As

---
24 *Genetic entropy* refers to the ongoing deterioration of the genetic code (genome) for any living thing.

a consequence, Darwin could articulate a scientific hypothesis that might have seemed reasonable in his time but should be recognized as being unreasonable today. Genetic mutations do occur, of course, and they can be beneficial. It is thought, as one example, that a small community in Italy has a mutant gene that counteracts the harmful effects of cholesterol in the blood.[25] So why couldn't life gradually evolve as a result of such mutations? The reason is that genetics does not work that way. Transformational advancement in life forms requires significant advancement in the genetic information of that life form. Such a phenomenon, however, appears to be impossible because the sum total of genetic mutations need to be, on balance, beneficial to the organism—something that doesn't happen. Damaging mutations overwhelmingly outnumber the good ones. Very few mutations are actually beneficial to the organism.[26] The genetic entropy argument says that because negative genetic mutations are far more numerous than the positive ones, our genetic code is continually deteriorating, not improving. And in the development of any organism, genetics is almost everything.

But evolutionists argue that natural selection eliminates the bad mutations by allowing the good ones to reproduce while the bad ones die off. Does that explain evolution? Prominent geneticist John Sanford[27] says it does not—the reason being that the bad mutations accumulate in the genetic code; many of them are not eliminated by natural selection. Every organism ends up having far more bad mutations than good ones, says Sanford, and these bad mutations are passed on to each new generation.[28]

Dr. Sanford has explained that every time a baby is born, that child has genetic information (the genome) that has been copied and merged from the genetic information of both parents. The genetic information of the parents, in turn, was copied and merged from their parents and so on. No genetic reproduction is perfect. Every time genetic information is copied and merged, more errors creep in. (A fertilized human ovum contains over three billion DNA base pairs of genetic

> Because negative genetic mutations are far more numerous than the positive ones, our genetic code is continually deteriorating, not improving.

---

25 Lee, "4 Beneficial Evolutionary Mutations."
26 Sanford, *Genetic Entropy*, 145–56.
27 Dr. Sanford is the author of more than eighty scientific publications and has been granted more than thirty patents dealing with genetics. He was largely responsible for creating the gene gun used for genetic engineering. Dr. Sanford has twice been awarded the Distinguished Inventor Award by the Central New York Patent Law Association, first in 1990 and again in 1995.
28 Sanford, *Genetic Entropy*, 137–40.

information.[29] It is not possible to perfectly replicate and merge these genetic base pairs without errors.)

To illustrate how this works, I conducted a simple experiment with a copy machine. In this experiment, I made twenty-five photocopies of a one-page paper. But instead of using the same original for all twenty-five copies, I used each new copy to create the next copy—as occurs in the transmission of genetic information from one generation to the next. After running twenty-five copies in this way, the results are striking. By the tenth copy, the lettering had become fuzzy. By the twentieth copy, the words were difficult to read. By the twenty-fifth copy, the page was not readable—so much inaccuracy had crept in that the final copy had no meaning at all. This experiment illustrates how genetics works: each new generation is a copy of the previous generation, and for that reason has more errors in its genetic code than the generation before. As a result, genetic problems are constantly being accumulated into our genetic code.

As a consequence, says Sanford, our genetic information is now riddled with errors. This is a major reason why people get arthritis. It is one of the reasons we get cancer and a primary reason we get Alzheimer's. It is the sole reason people get hemophilia, Huntington's disease, sickle-cell anemia, and a host of other maladies. According to Sanford, it is common knowledge in the field of genetics that the human genome is constantly deteriorating. Modern medicine and good nutrition can offset the consequences of these genetic maladies—for a time and to a degree—but this doesn't change the fact that the genome continues to go downhill.[30]

Anyone who wishes to test Dr. Sanford's conclusions should do an Internet search for "negative human mutations" and another search for "positive human mutations." The list of negative mutations will be long and impressive. The list of positive mutations will be short and questionable. The list of positive mutations is suspect because it includes alleged mutations like perfect pitch and unusual artistic ability—characteristics that are likely part of the normal human genome. There is no reason to believe that such talents are mutations.

---

29 National Institutes of Health, "What Is a Genome?"
30 This is why close relatives should not marry. The children of close relatives are likely to exhibit the mutations carried as recessive genes by their parents. If most mutations were positive, then the children of close relatives should be genetically superior to their parents. As we know, however, the opposite is true. The children of close relatives display a host of genetic maladies, the reason being that we all carry far more negative mutations than positive. Many of these negative mutations will be revealed in the offspring when close relatives marry and recessive genes are then allowed to manifest themselves.

All this means that Darwin's central explanation of how evolution supposedly works is now known to be false. The human genome has been deteriorating from the beginning, not advancing. At the same time, however, few members of the public know this is so. Few people have been informed that Darwin's central explanatory thesis is now known to be false.

This information points to the existence of a Creator God. We would expect that life created by God would be perfect at the time of creation. It is reasonable that genetic information could deteriorate with time, and Genesis says that life became corrupted as a consequence of sin entering the world. For these reasons, the well-documented contamination of the genetic code points to a Creator God while it also disproves the central thesis of Darwinian evolution.

It would be difficult to overstate the importance of Sanford's research. Our culture continually asserts that human beings are improving. We are frequently told that before long, our life span will be well over one hundred years. We are told that our intelligence has steadily increased from that of Neanderthal man to Cro-Magnon man up to modern man—though archaeological information at hand says the opposite. The truth is, from the standpoint of genetics at least, we are in an ongoing state of decline, not improvement. An objective and honest study of the history of human beings, as well as an honest study of all of nature, shows this to be so. For example, both Neanderthal man and Cro-Magnon man are known to have had larger brains, and presumably greater mental capacity, than modern man as well as having been physically superior as well.[31]

Hebrews 11:3 clarifies that creation of the world out of nothing by a personal God is a matter of faith.

We keep in mind, however, that arguments like these do not lead us to God as we know Him. The arguments leave open numerous possibilities. Nature could be God. Polytheism could be true. The Deists could be correct that God started things rolling and then excused Himself from further involvement in what He had started.

In addition, it's important to note that neither general revelation nor science can definitively prove that a God of any kind created the universe and life in it. Science can only describe how nature normally works, and the creation of life

---

31 Fran Dorey, "*Homo Neanderthalensis* - The Neanderthals," Australian Museum, last updated October 30, 2015, https://australianmuseum.net.au/homo-neanderthalensis, and Lisa Zyga, "Cro Magnon Skull Shows That Our Brains Have Shrunk," *PhysOrg.com*, March 15, 2010, https://phys.org/news/2010-03-cro-magnon-skull-brains-shrunk.html.

out of nothing is clearly an exception to the norm. These four arguments do suggest, however, that we need more than matter and energy to explain what we see. That something more, Christians believe, is God.

Because these arguments only take us to a life force of some kind, or a God or gods of some kind, Hebrews 11:3 clarifies that creation of the world out of nothing by a personal God is a matter of faith. The greatest truths of our existence can be known only by God revealing Himself to us—through the truths in His Word; in critically important events in human history, such as the miraculous crossing of the Red Sea by the Israelites; and in His Son, Jesus Christ. The next chapters will examine how God has revealed Himself to us and how He has given us compelling evidence to demonstrate that the Bible really is God Himself speaking.

QUESTIONS FOR REVIEW AND DISCUSSION

1. Various opinion polls suggest that as our knowledge of the universe grows, the percentage of our population who believe in God declines. Why might this be?

2. Traditionally, science has been defined as obtaining knowledge by means of observation. Today, however, science is often defined from the viewpoint of philosophical naturalism, also called materialism, which is the view that the universe consists of nature plus nothing—nature is all there is. Not surprisingly, those who define science this way end up concluding that God does not exist and adopting evolution because, as they see it, the alternative (special creation) is impossible. As Christians, how should we deal with this new definition of science?

CHAPTER 4

GOD REVEALED

As noted above, the greatest truths of our existence can be known only by God revealing Himself to us, as He did through His many prophets and as recorded in the Holy Scriptures. Many other individuals, however, such as Muhammad (AD 570–632), have also claimed to be prophets of God, whom Muhammad called "Allah." How can we distinguish between those prophets who were genuine, if any, and those making false claims?

We saw in chapter 2 that the apostles explained several objective criteria people were encouraged to use to identify true prophets. The New Testament apostles described closely related criteria that identified Jesus of Nazareth as not only a true prophet of God but also much more: the Messiah of God. They did so by (1) describing many sensational miracles performed by Jesus and the apostles themselves, (2) explaining that Jesus fulfilled the Old Testament messianic prophecies, (3) highlighting the resurrection of Jesus from the dead, and (4) verifying the reality of Jesus' resurrection by the testimony of numerous eyewitnesses who, in their martyrdom, signed their testimony in their own blood. In the same way, those living before the coming of Christ were given similar objective criteria for identifying both the true God and is genuine prophets. One such criterion was this: the real God has verified His genuineness by means of the extraordinary miracles He has performed Himself and through His true prophets. Many of these miracles are recorded for us in the Old Testament.

THE PARTING OF THE RED SEA

One of God's most sensational miracles was the Israelite's crossing of the Red Sea on dry ground while the pursuing Egyptian army was completely destroyed. The Book of Exodus tells us the impact this miracle had on the people of Israel. It reads as follows:

> Thus the LORD saved Israel that day from the hand of the Egyptians, and Israel saw the Egyptians dead on the seashore. Israel saw the great power that the LORD used against the Egyptians, so the people feared the LORD, and they believed in the LORD and in His servant Moses. (14:30–31)

It is certainly reasonable that the Israelites would recognize the Lord God as the only true God after witnessing such an astonishing miracle. We observe that, based on this miracle, the people also recognized Moses as being God's prophet.

The impact this miracle had on at least some non-Israelites is also significant. When, some forty years later, the Israelite spies in Jericho were welcomed and protected by Rahab, a prostitute, she explained to them why she, too, was a believer in the Lord God. This is what she said:

> Before the men lay down, she came up to them on the roof and said to the men, "I know that the LORD has given you the land, and that the fear of you has fallen upon us, and that all the inhabitants of the land melt away before you. For we have heard how the LORD dried up the water of the Red Sea before you when you came out of Egypt, and what you did to the two kings of the Amorites who were beyond the Jordan, to Sihon and Og, whom you devoted to destruction. And as soon as we heard it, our hearts melted, and there was no spirit left in any man because of you, for the LORD your God, He is God in the heavens above and on the earth beneath. Now then, please swear to me by the LORD that, as I have dealt kindly with you, you also will deal kindly with my father's house, and give me a sure sign that you will save alive my father and mother, my brothers and sisters, and all who belong to them, and deliver our lives from death." And the men said to her, "Our life for yours even to death! If you do not tell this business of ours, then when the LORD gives us the land we will deal kindly and faithfully with you." (Joshua 2:8–14)

For most of recorded human history, unbelievers generally believed that each nation had its own god or gods. There were the gods of the Egyptians, the gods of the Canaanites, the gods of the Amorites, even gods of the Israelites, and so on. But when Rahab learned of the spectacular miracles accomplished by the God of the Israelites, she concluded that their God was the only real God. It was obvious to her that these other supposed gods were not real, but the Lord God was. She confessed to the spies that "the LORD your

God, He is God in the heavens above and on the earth beneath" (v. 11). That is, Rahab recognized that this notion of each nation having its own god or gods was not true. She knew it was untrue because the Lord God had demonstrated that He was God over everything, from the heavens above to the earth below, including being the God of all the nations. In this way, God's revelation of who He is by means of His miracles led Rahab to a saving faith in Him. She demonstrated the reality of her faith by protecting the spies.

Examples such as this, which explain how God revealed and authenticated Himself through His miracles, abound in the Old Testament.

GOD VS. THE PROPHETS OF BAAL

Another remarkable miracle took place some 550 years after the crossing of the Red Sea. Once again, the Lord God demonstrated beyond all doubt that He is the one and only genuine God. The Lord God additionally revealed Elijah to be His true prophet through a miraculous event. This miracle is recorded in 1 Kings 18:20–40:

> So Ahab sent to all the people of Israel and gathered the prophets together at Mount Carmel. And Elijah came near to all the people and said, "How long will you go limping between two different opinions? If the LORD is God, follow Him; but if Baal, then follow him." And the people did not answer him a word. Then Elijah said to the people, "I, even I only, am left a prophet of the LORD, but Baal's prophets are 450 men. Let two bulls be given to us, and let them choose one bull for themselves and cut it in pieces and lay it on the wood, but put no fire to it. And I will prepare the other bull and lay it on the wood and put no fire to it. And you call upon the name of your god, and I will call upon the name of the LORD, and the God who answers by fire, he is God." And all the people answered, "It is well spoken." Then Elijah said to the prophets of Baal, "Choose for yourselves one bull and prepare it first, for you are many, and call upon the name of your god, but put no fire to it." And they took the bull that was given them, and they prepared it and called upon the name of Baal from morning until noon, saying, "O Baal, answer us!" But there was no voice, and no one answered. And they limped around the altar that they had made. And at noon Elijah mocked them, saying, "Cry aloud, for he is a god. Either he is musing, or he is relieving himself, or he is on a journey, or perhaps he is asleep and must be awakened." And they cried aloud and cut themselves after their custom with

swords and lances, until the blood gushed out upon them. And as midday passed, they raved on until the time of the offering of the oblation, but there was no voice. No one answered; no one paid attention.

Then Elijah said to all the people, "Come near to me." And all the people came near to him. And he repaired the altar of the LORD that had been thrown down. Elijah took twelve stones, according to the number of the tribes of the sons of Jacob, to whom the word of the LORD came, saying, "Israel shall be your name," and with the stones he built an altar in the name of the LORD. And he made a trench about the altar, as great as would contain two seahs of seed. And he put the wood in order and cut the bull in pieces and laid it on the wood. And he said, "Fill four jars with water and pour it on the burnt offering and on the wood." And he said, "Do it a second time." And they did it a second time. And he said, "Do it a third time." And they did it a third time. And the water ran around the altar and filled the trench also with water.

And at the time of the offering of the oblation, Elijah the prophet came near and said, "O LORD, God of Abraham, Isaac, and Israel, let it be known this day that You are God in Israel, and that I am Your servant, and that I have done all these things at Your word. Answer me, O LORD, answer me, that this people may know that You, O LORD, are God, and that You have turned their hearts back." Then the fire of the LORD fell and consumed the burnt offering and the wood and the stones and the dust, and licked up the water that was in the trench. And when all the people saw it, they fell on their faces and said, "The LORD, He is God; the LORD, He is God." And Elijah said to them, "Seize the prophets of Baal; let not one of them escape." And they seized them. And Elijah brought them down to the brook Kishon and slaughtered them there.

Once again, the Lord God demonstrated in a powerful way that He is the true God while Baal was a false god who could do nothing because he doesn't exist. Elijah prayed as follows: "Answer me, O LORD, answer me, that this people may know that You, O LORD, are God, and that You have turned their hearts back" (v. 37). And the people responded to the miracle by saying: "The LORD, He is God; the LORD, He is God" (v. 39). God used this miracle to strengthen the faith of His people and to create faith in the hearts of those who had not been believers. We can see that in Old Testament times, faith

Blind leaps of faith are not found in the Old Testament, nor are they found in the New Testament.

was not a blind leap of some kind. Faith in the Lord God was grounded in good and sufficient evidence—on objective evidence that was there for all to see.

This miracle additionally established Elijah as a true prophet of God—someone chosen by God to speak on His behalf. The widow of Zarephath understood this verification process as revealed by her statement to Elijah after he raised her son from the dead. She said: "Now I know that you are a man of God, and that the word of the LORD in your mouth is truth" (1 Kings 17:24). We see, therefore, that the Lord God provided such miracles largely to provide concrete, historical evidence that He is the only true God and also to establish His prophets as being genuine. Blind leaps of faith are not found in the Old Testament, nor are they found in the New Testament, as we have seen.

In Old Testament times, and in our time, there have been and still are a myriad of competing religious voices coming from those who claim to have the truth. How could the Israelite nation, and how can we, determine who can be trusted and who cannot? For this, God gave His people four clear and objective criteria to identify those prophets who are telling the truth and those who are not. We now turn to these criteria.

FOUR CRITERIA OF TRUE PROPHETS

The ability to perform miracles like those mentioned above was an important guideline for identifying true prophets. There were, however, other standards as well. The Old Testament actually explains four guidelines the Israelites were instructed to use to distinguish between true prophets and false ones. They are as follows:

1. TRUE PROPHETS WERE OFTEN ENABLED TO PERFORM SENSATIONAL MIRACLES.

The miracles described above exemplify this criterion. One more example involves the signs God gave Moses to establish his credibility before Pharaoh. God gave Moses these instructions:

> Then Moses answered, "But behold, they will not believe me or listen to my voice, for they will say, 'The LORD did not appear to you.'" The LORD said to him, "What is that in your hand?" He said, "A staff." And He said, "Throw it on the ground." So he threw it on the ground, and it became a serpent, and Moses ran from it. But the LORD said to Moses, "Put out your hand and catch it by

the tail"—so he put out his hand and caught it, and it became a staff in his hand—"that they may believe that the Lord, the God of their fathers, the God of Abraham, the God of Isaac, and the God of Jacob, has appeared to you." (Exodus 4:1–5)

This sign, along with many others, should have enabled Pharaoh and his court to conclude that Moses was a true prophet of the Lord God. Such miracles additionally demonstrated that the Lord God is the only genuine God. The importance of this miracle, and the many other miracles Moses performed, is well summarized by the following statement from Deuteronomy:

> And there has not arisen a prophet since in Israel like Moses, whom the Lord knew face to face, none like him for all the signs and the wonders that the Lord sent him to do in the land of Egypt, to Pharaoh and to all his servants and to all his land, and for all the mighty power and all the great deeds of terror that Moses did in the sight of all Israel. (34:10–12)

Moses was succeeded by Joshua, and God demonstrated to His people that Joshua, too, was a true prophet like Moses. We read from the Book of Joshua:

> The Lord said to Joshua, "Today I will begin to exalt you in the sight of all Israel, that they may know that, as I was with Moses, so I will be with you. And as for you, command the priests who bear the ark of the covenant, 'When you come to the brink of the waters of the Jordan, you shall stand still in the Jordan.'" And Joshua said to the people of Israel, "Come here and listen to the words of the Lord your God." And Joshua said, "Here is how you shall know that the living God is among you and that he will without fail drive out from before you the Canaanites, the Hittites, the Hivites, the Perizzites, the Girgashites, the Amorites, and the Jebusites. Behold, the ark of the covenant of the Lord of all the earth is passing over before you into the Jordan. Now therefore take twelve men from the tribes of Israel, from each tribe a man. And when the soles of the feet of the priests bearing the ark of the Lord, the Lord of all the earth, shall rest in the waters of the Jordan, the waters of the Jordan shall be cut off from flowing, and the waters coming down from above shall stand in one heap."

> So when the people set out from their tents to pass over the Jordan with the priests bearing the ark of the covenant before the

people, and as soon as those bearing the ark had come as far as the Jordan, and the feet of the priests bearing the ark were dipped in the brink of the water (now the Jordan overflows all its banks throughout the time of harvest), the waters coming down from above stood and rose up in a heap very far away, at Adam, the city that is beside Zarethan, and those flowing down toward the Sea of the Arabah, the Salt Sea, were completely cut off. And the people passed over opposite Jericho. Now the priests bearing the ark of the covenant of the Lord stood firmly on dry ground in the midst of the Jordan, and all Israel was passing over on dry ground until all the nation finished passing over the Jordan. (3:7–17)

Just as Moses had been established as a true prophet by a great miracle, in the same way Joshua was established as a true prophet by a great miracle. Not all the prophets of God were recorded as having done miracles, but many of them were. And as noted above, it is not surprising that when the woman at the well of Sychar recognized that Jesus was illustrating supernatural knowledge about her past, she responded by saying: "Sir, I perceive that You are a prophet" (John 4:19). And when the man born blind whom Jesus had healed was asked about Jesus' identity, he understandably replied, "He is a prophet" (John 9:17). We can see, therefore, that the people of the Old Testament, up to and including the time of Jesus, understood that the ability to work miracles was a sign of a true prophet, and the people of that time applied this criterion without hesitation.

One of Jesus' sensational miracles, as mentioned above, was His healing of a man born blind. Jesus' enemies were at a loss to explain away a miracle such as this. Part of their attempt to find an explanation is recorded below. To the man who had been healed, they said:

"We know that God has spoken to Moses, but as for this man, we do not know where He comes from." The man answered, "Why, this is an amazing thing! You do not know where He comes from, and yet He opened my eyes. We know that God does not listen to sinners, but if anyone is a worshiper of God and does His will, God listens to him. Never since the world began has it been heard that anyone opened the eyes of a man born blind. If this man were not from God, He could do nothing." (John 9:29–33)

The man born blind properly concluded that a miracle of this magnitude could only be done by God Himself. This truth in part explains why Jesus' enemies became desperate after He raised Lazarus from the dead.

They lamented, "If we let Him go on like this, everyone will believe in Him" (John 11:48). These Jewish leaders knew that Moses had prophesied about the coming of *the prophet* who would be like him but greater (Deuteronomy 18:15–20). It would have been difficult for these Jewish leaders not to recognize that the miracles being performed by Jesus identified Him as the prophet predicted by Moses. These leaders either had to recognize Jesus as such or do something desperate as quickly as possible.

2. TRUE PROPHETS AGREED WITH THE TEACHING OF MOSES.

Once Moses had been identified as a true prophet of God, and once the Lord God had been established as the one true God, it then followed that other true prophets would advocate allegiance to the Lord God alone and would teach the same doctrines as Moses. Based on this principle, Moses instructed the Israelites as follows:

> "If a prophet or a dreamer of dreams arises among you and gives you a sign or a wonder, and the sign or wonder that he tells you comes to pass, and if he says, 'Let us go after other gods,' which you have not known, 'and let us serve them' you shall not listen to the words of that prophet or that dreamer of dreams. For the LORD your God is testing you, to know whether you love the LORD your God with all your heart and with all your soul. You shall walk after the LORD your God and fear Him and keep His commandments and obey His voice, and you shall serve Him and hold fast to Him. But that prophet or that dreamer of dreams shall be put to death, because he has taught rebellion against the LORD your God, who brought you out of the land of Egypt and redeemed you out of the house of slavery, to make you leave the way in which the LORD your God commanded you to walk." (Deuteronomy 13:1–5)

An underlying assumption for this command was that, by itself, performing miracles or the illusion of miracles was not sufficient proof that someone was a true prophet of God. Satan, too, can accomplish miraculous signs to a limited degree. When Moses appeared before Pharaoh and his court, Pharaoh's magicians could also perform miracles albeit of a lesser magnitude than the signs of Moses. In addition, it may be that false prophets could make accurate predictions just by chance some of the time. In addition, the Holy Spirit may have on occasion used Jesus' enemies to make accurate statements because it suited His purposes, as is seen in John 18:14, which reads: "It was Caiaphas who had advised the Jews that it would be expedient that one man should die for the people."

Similarly, in our day, it appears that persons with familiar spirits (fallen angels serving Satan) can describe realities or events about which they should have no knowledge.[32] It seems that they do so by the powers of the underworld. See, for example, the book *Seth Speaks: The Eternal Validity of the Soul* by Jane Roberts, as well as other Seth books. It looks like the powers of darkness can do some inexplicable things, but they cannot predict the future with any consistency, and the miracles done by God's power are far more wondrous than Satan's miracles. We must apply the biblical criteria for true prophets in our day too. Anyone who teaches contrary to the writings of Moses is to be identified as a false prophet.

Jesus' enemies were well aware of the principle that simply working miracles was not enough to establish someone as a true prophet of God. They knew that true prophets must also teach in accordance with the writings of Moses, and they attempted to use this criteria to discredit Jesus. Matthew 19:3 records such an attempt: "And Pharisees came up to Him and tested Him by asking, 'Is it lawful to divorce one's wife for any cause?'" These enemies of Jesus knew He had previously said that divorce, except for the cause of adultery, was wrong (Matthew 5:31–32). They hoped, therefore, that Jesus would either contradict what Moses said or contradict Himself. Either way, Jesus would be discredited.

Jesus, however, understood the law much better than the Pharisees, and He responded as follows: "Because of your hardness of heart Moses allowed you to divorce your wives, but from the beginning it was not so. And I say to you: whoever divorces his wife, except for sexual immorality, and marries another, commits adultery" (Matthew 19:8–9). In this way, Jesus clarified that there was no contradiction between what He and Moses had said because Moses was speaking of the civil law—which cannot prohibit all immoral acts—while Jesus was speaking of the moral law, which stipulated that divorce without just cause was wrong. As a consequence, Jesus not only demonstrated that He taught in agreement with Moses, but He additionally revealed that He understood what Moses had said much better than His enemies.

3. THE PREDICTIONS OF TRUE PROPHETS ALWAYS CAME TO PASS.

The task of a prophet was not primarily that of predicting the future. His task was speaking to the people on God's behalf. Such speaking, however, commonly involved future events. These predictions provided other criteria whereby the genuineness of prophets could be evaluated. It was mandatory

---

32   See Acts 16:16–18.

that the predictions of prophets came true. Jeremiah said: "The prophet who prophesies peace, when the word of that prophet comes to pass, then it will be known that the Lord has truly sent the prophet" (Jeremiah 28:9).

The Old Testament contains numerous prophecies that were fulfilled during the lifetime of the prophets. One such example is recorded in the Book of Daniel as he interpreted the handwriting on the wall for King Belshazzar. Daniel's interpretation reads as follows:

> "And you his son, Belshazzar, have not humbled your heart, though you knew all this, but you have lifted up yourself against the Lord of heaven. And the vessels of his house have been brought in before you, and you and your lords, your wives, and your concubines have drunk wine from them. And you have praised the gods of silver and gold, of bronze, iron, wood, and stone, which do not see or hear or know, but the God in whose hand is your breath, and whose are all your ways, you have not honored.
>
> "Then from his presence the hand was sent, and this writing was inscribed. And this is the writing that was inscribed: Mene, Mene, Tekel, and Parsin. This is the interpretation of the matter: Mene, God has numbered the days of your kingdom and brought it to an end; Tekel, you have been weighed in the balances and found wanting; Peres, your kingdom is divided and given to the Medes and Persians."
>
> Then Belshazzar gave the command, and Daniel was clothed with purple, a chain of gold was put around his neck, and a proclamation was made about him, that he should be the third ruler in the kingdom.
>
> That very night Belshazzar the Chaldean king was killed. And Darius the Mede received the kingdom, being about sixty-two years old. (Daniel 5:22–31)

The supernatural knowledge displayed here by Daniel, as well as the fulfillment of his prophecy so quickly after he made it, clearly identified him as a true prophet of God.

Another fulfilled prophecy in the Old Testament is recorded in Deuteronomy 30:15–20. Moses said:

> See, I have set before you today life and good, death and evil. If you obey the commandments of the Lord your God that I command you today, by loving the Lord your God, by walking in His

ways, and by keeping His commandments and His statutes and His rules, then you shall live and multiply, and the Lord your God will bless you in the land that you are entering to take possession of it. But if your heart turns away, and you will not hear, but are drawn away to worship other gods and serve them, I declare to you today, that you shall surely perish. You shall not live long in the land that you are going over the Jordan to enter and possess. I call heaven and earth to witness against you today, that I have set before you life and death, blessing and curse. Therefore choose life, that you and your offspring may live, loving the Lord your God, obeying His voice and holding fast to Him, for He is your life and length of days, that you may dwell in the land that the Lord swore to your fathers, to Abraham, to Isaac, and to Jacob, to give them."

In this way, Moses essentially predicted that when the Israelites were on the Lord God's side and followed His commands, they would succeed, but when they followed other gods, they would fail. The Israelites' history up until and including the time of Christ demonstrated again and again that this prophecy was true.[33] We notice that Moses ended this prophecy with the promise of God's blessing when Israel returned to being faithful to Him.

The Old Testament contains numerous prophecies that were fulfilled during the lifetimes of the prophets, enough for their contemporaries to identify them as genuine prophets. Some of the prophecies, however, were not fulfilled until later. Many of them were not fulfilled until the coming of the Messiah. One such prediction was proclaimed by the prophet Micah:

> But you, O Bethlehem Ephrathah,
>   who are too little to be among the clans of Judah,
> from you shall come forth for Me
>   one who is to be ruler in Israel,
> whose coming forth is from of old,
>   from ancient days. (Micah 5:2)

This prediction enabled the Jewish rabbis to tell King Herod and the Wise Men that the Messiah would be born in Bethlehem (Matthew 2:4–6). We should recognize that the fulfillment of these messianic prophecies gives us a substantial advantage in identifying true prophets, an advantage those who lived before the coming of Christ did not have. We have the benefit of

---

33 See 2 Kings 17:7–8.

seeing the fulfillment of the messianic prophecies in Jesus, the Christ, a reality that gives us even greater confidence that the prophetic writings we have are authentic.[34]

4. TRUE PROPHETS AVOID THE MARKS OF FALSE PROPHETS.

The Old Testament not only provides us with the criteria for identifying true prophets, but it also describes the characteristics of false prophets. Following are the marks of false prophets as described by the true prophets of the Old Testament time:

(a) *False prophets tell the people what they want to hear.* The prophet Micah explained this characteristic as follows: "If a man should go about and utter wind and lies, saying, 'I will preach to you of wine and strong drink,' he would be the preacher for this people!" (Micah 2:11). (See also 2 Chronicles 18.)

(b) *False prophets make predictions that are self-serving.* We read from Micah again: "Thus says the LORD concerning the prophets who lead My people astray, who can cry 'Peace' when they have something to eat, but declare war against him who puts nothing into their mouths" (Micah 3:5).

(c) *False prophets promote gods other than the true God.* The prophet Jeremiah said:

> In the prophets of Samaria
> I saw an unsavory thing:
> they prophesied by Baal
> and led My people Israel astray. (Jeremiah 23:13)

(d) *False prophets lead immoral lives.* Jeremiah declared:

> But in the prophets of Jerusalem
> I have seen a horrible thing:
> they commit adultery and walk in lies;
> they strengthen the hands of evildoers,
> so that no one turns from his evil;
> all of them have become like Sodom to me,
> and its inhabitants like Gomorrah. (Jeremiah 23:14)

(e) *False prophets make predictions that do not come true.* Ezekiel described them as follows:

> Therefore thus says the Lord GOD: "Because you have

---

34 See 2 Peter 1:19.

> uttered falsehood and seen lying visions, therefore behold, I am against you, declares the Lord GOD. My hand will be against the prophets who see false visions and who give lying divinations." (Ezekiel 13:8–9)

As we can see, these criteria for distinguishing true prophets from false are detailed, reasonable, and verifiable. They required the Israelites to make rational decisions based on the above criteria to determine to whom they should listen and whom they should avoid. This is not to say that the Israelites always followed these criteria. They often did not, to their detriment. Nevertheless, the Israelites had the standards at their disposal, which were intended to keep them on the right path.

We can see, therefore, that for Old Testament believers, as well as for New Testament Christians, faith was not a blind leap into the unknown. The Christian faith has always been based on verifiable history. It has always been based on objective criteria and upon information and evidence relating to those criteria. No other religion can make such a claim.

IS THE OLD TESTAMENT ACCURATE?

The criteria for identifying true prophets of God outlined above were objective, reasonable, and sufficient for allowing the Israelites to distinguish between true and false prophets. We who live now, however, employ additional criteria, one being the question of whether the biblical accounts are in agreement with other verifiable information, including archaeological discoveries. There is no reason why the normal criteria used by historians to authenticate documents shouldn't be applied to our Old Testament documents. In addition, the apostle Paul gave us a precedent for this kind of analysis when he said to Agrippa, "'For the king knows about these things, and to him I speak boldly. For I am persuaded that none of these things has escaped his notice, for this has not been done in a corner'" (Acts 26:26). That is, Paul appealed to the secular accounts Agrippa would have had available to him to verify the accuracy of his own testimony.

> The Christian faith has always been based on verifiable history. . . . No other religion can make such a claim.

ARCHAEOLOGICAL EVIDENCE

How well do biblical records correspond to other information at our disposal?

In answer, it is fair to say that we now have extensive archaeological confirmation of the accuracy of much of the Old Testament historical and geographical detail—such as the mention of the cities of Sodom and Gomorrah in the passage above from Jeremiah 23. Up until relatively recent times, skeptics argued that the cities of Sodom and Gomorrah never existed because no mention of them could be found apart from the Old and New Testaments. But the discovery of the Ebla Tablets in 1974 refuted this view. These tablets, among other things, include records of trade arrangements between the city of Ebla and the cities of Sodom and Gomorrah. Dr. Clifford Wilson commented on the content of the Ebla tablets as follows:

> Two of the towns mentioned are Sodom and Gomorrah. Here we are transported back to about 2,300 B.C., and we find that these towns were regularly visited, being on the route of the King's Highway that ran down from Damascus. There are actually references to five "cities of the Plain" (to use the Biblical term at Genesis 14:2), and these were Sodom, Gomorrah, Admah, Zeboiim, and Zoar. We are told in that same verse that an earlier name for Zoar was Bela.[35]

In addition to the Ebla tablets, the Greek historian Strabo (64 BC–AD 24) wrote that Sodom was the metropolis for thirteen cities located in the region of Masada (an ancient city near the Dead Sea).[36]

There are hundreds, if not thousands, of examples where archaeological and other research has confirmed the accuracy of the Old Testament. For example, take the archaeological discovery of substantial supplies of wheat that were in storage when the city of Jericho fell to the Israelite army. Normally, a besieged city would exhaust its food supply before being taken, but the Book of Joshua informs us that Jericho fell in just a few days[37] (Joshua 6:1–20). The Book of Joshua also informs us that Jericho was set on fire after its capture (Joshua 6:24), a fact of history that has also been confirmed by archaeological research.[38] All that said, the discovery of charred wheat in watertight pottery containers was not all that surprising—for if wheat is kept dry, as it was in the clay containers, it will last many thousands of years.

Not only has modern research confirmed much of the biblical narrative, it is fair to say that no biblical record has been shown to be in error. Few, if any, ancient records have been shown to be as trustworthy.

> There are hundreds, if not thousands, of examples where archaeological and other research has confirmed the accuracy of the Old Testament.

---

35   Wilson, "Ebla."
36   *New World Encyclopedia.*
37   Petrovich, "Battle for the Bible" (lecture).
38   Petrovich, "Battle for the Bible" (lecture).

> Not only has modern research confirmed much of the biblical narrative, it is fair to say that no biblical record has been shown to be in error.

THE VERBAL INSPIRATION OF THE OLD TESTAMENT

Even though this book focuses on apologetics, on evidence for the Christian faith, matters of doctrine are often interconnected with those of evidence. The Bible clearly states that writings of the Old Testament prophets are the result of inspiration by God the Holy Spirit. And if the Old Testament was inspired by God, it is also inerrant. Accordingly, Peter said, "For no prophecy was ever produced by the will of man, but men spoke from God as they were carried along by the Holy Spirit" (2 Peter 1:21).

So how do we know that the Old Testament Scriptures were given to us by God's inspiration? We know this to be true because the Bible says it is true. This line of thought, while accurate, can raise questions, however. It appears to be a circular argument. Some may reply that this apparent circularity doesn't matter because it's the Holy Spirit who convinces us that the Bible is inspired, not logic. This is true, but there is also more to be said.

We are speaking here of the argument recorded in 2 Peter 1:16–21, which reads as follows:

> For we did not follow cleverly devised myths when we made known to you the power and coming of our Lord Jesus Christ, but we were eyewitnesses of His majesty. For when He received honor and glory from God the Father, and the voice was borne to Him by the Majestic Glory, "This is my beloved Son, with whom I am well pleased," we ourselves heard this very voice borne from heaven, for we were with Him on the holy mountain. And we have the prophetic word more fully confirmed, to which you will do well to pay attention as to a lamp shining in a dark place, until the day dawns and the morning star rises in your hearts, knowing this first of all, that no prophecy of Scripture comes from someone's own interpretation. For no prophecy was ever produced by the will of man, but men spoke from God as they were carried along by the Holy Spirit.

In this statement, it is evident that Peter was not only explaining the doctrine of verbal inspiration, he was additionally making a clear and powerful argument that the doctrine of the verbal inspiration of the Old Testament is true. Peter began by proving that

1. *Jesus is the Christ of God.* As evidence, Peter said that he and several other disciples were with Jesus when He was transfigured before them; they saw Him in all His glory as God Almighty. Look how

Peter emphasized that they were eyewitnesses of all this. Peter stated that with their own ears they heard God say that Jesus was His "beloved Son with whom I am well pleased." Again, look at how Peter emphasized that they saw this with their own eyes and heard it with their own ears. Having demonstrated that Jesus is the promised Messiah, Peter then proceeded to his second conclusion:

2. *Since we know that Jesus is the promised Messiah, we also know that the prophets who predicted His coming were true prophets of God.* Chapter 7 will enumerate many of the messianic prophecies that Jesus fulfilled. Peter's readers were familiar with these messianic prophecies and how Jesus completed them. The Old Testament believers could not have seen this fulfillment, but the New Testament believers did. Peter here appealed to the well-known tests for true prophets and boldly stated, "We have the prophetic word more fully confirmed" (v. 19). That is, the messianic predictions of the prophets have now been fulfilled in Jesus Christ. For that reason, we have even greater confidence that the prophets we have been trusting are genuine prophets of God. This brings us to Peter's primary conclusion.

3. *Therefore, the Old Testament prophets were writing under the direction of the Holy Spirit.* We know this to be the true because only God knows the future and, therefore, only God could have told the prophets what the future holds. The only way the prophets could have made these now-fulfilled messianic predictions was by writing under God's direction.

We can see, therefore, that not only did Peter say the prophets were inspired by God the Holy Spirit, but he also made a powerful argument for the truth of his statement. His argument is based on premises that are well-substantiated, making his conclusion valid. This means the doctrine the Old Testament prophets wrote by inspiration of God is not circular at all. It is actually a valid, sophisticated, and well-supported deductive argument. It would be difficult to challenge the truth of Peter's conclusion. This is the kind of argument an attorney would love to have in a court of law. An argument like this decides the case in your favor.

Yes, Christianity is a matter of faith, and yes, verbal inspiration is ultimately a matter of faith. But verbal inspiration is a matter of faith based on genuine history, on objective evidence. The information available, including the information summarized in this book, makes a strong case that God actually has revealed Himself to us. He has done so in real-life history. He has

Yes, Christianity is a matter of faith, and yes, verbal inspiration is ultimately a matter of faith. But verbal inspiration is a matter of faith based on genuine history, on objective evidence.

done so in a manner that allows His revelation to be evaluated and verified by objective evidence that most anyone has the opportunity to examine if they wish. They can do so, for example, by investigating the accuracy of the biblical record as is done in this work. The Bible actually instructs us to put it, as well as anyone who claims to speak religious truth, to the test. As John says: "Beloved, do not believe every spirit, but test the spirits to see whether they are from God, for many false prophets have gone out into the world" (1 John 4:1).[39] And the Bible additionally provides us with objective and reasonable criteria to be used in evaluating any writing or person who claims to have spiritual truth. When we do so, we will see that God has revealed Himself to us in a manner that allows us to see the certainty of the truth of His revelation.

QUESTIONS FOR REVIEW AND DISCUSSION

1. Can you think of a way the criteria for identifying true prophets could have been improved? What additional criteria should have been added?

2. Are those who say they don't believe the Bible actually taking a blind leap of faith away from Christianity? How might you respond to someone who says this?

---

39   Essentially the same exhortation is contained in Isaiah 40–41.

CHAPTER 5

JESUS, THE MASTER TEACHER AND MESSIAH

We now turn to the greatest prophet of all, the prophet who claimed to be God in the flesh, Jesus of Nazareth. The same criteria we applied to other prophets can be applied to Jesus as well. In the case of Jesus, however, there is another important criterion that comes into play, that being the standard of consistency. And there are many who agree that Jesus was a great man, a great teacher, a prophet perhaps, but do not agree that He is God in the flesh. Islam, for example, subscribes to this view. But is this a reasonable position to hold? C. S. Lewis answered this question as follows:

> I am trying here to prevent anyone saying the really foolish thing that people often say about Him: I'm ready to accept Jesus as a great moral teacher, but I don't accept His claim to be God. That is the one thing we must not say. A man who was merely a man and said the sort of things Jesus said would not be a great moral teacher. He would either be a lunatic—on the level with the man who says he is a poached egg—or else he would be the Devil of Hell. You must make your choice. Either this man was, and is, the Son of God, or else a madman or something worse. You can shut Him up for a fool, you can spit at Him and kill Him as a demon or you can fall at His feet and call Him Lord and God, but let us not come with any patronizing nonsense about His being a great human teacher. He has not left that open to us. He did not intend to.[40]

---

[40] Lewis, *Mere Christianity*, 55–56. Copyright © C. S. Lewis Pte. Ltd. 1942, 1943, 1944, 1952. Extract reprinted by permission.

Lewis is correct in the alternatives he describes. The criterion of consistency requires these two options: Either Jesus was living in fantasy, was a liar or worse, or otherwise He is exactly who He said He was, God in the flesh. Which was He? Evaluating the way Jesus taught the crowds of people who followed Him will answer that question for us—for the manner in which a teacher carries out his mission reveals, to a large extent, who he is.

THE PARABLE OF THE GOOD SAMARITAN

The historian Luke described for us one of Jesus' best-known teaching sessions, that being His parable of the Good Samaritan. It reads as follows:

> And behold, a lawyer stood up to put Him to the test, saying, "Teacher, what shall I do to inherit eternal life?" He said to him, "What is written in the Law? How do you read it?" And he answered, "You shall love the Lord your God with all your heart and with all your soul and with all your strength and with all your mind, and your neighbor as yourself." And He said to him, "You have answered correctly; do this, and you will live."
>
> But he, desiring to justify himself, said to Jesus, "And who is my neighbor?" Jesus replied, "A man was going down from Jerusalem to Jericho, and he fell among robbers, who stripped him and beat him and departed, leaving him half dead. Now by chance a priest was going down that road, and when he saw him he passed by on the other side. So likewise a Levite, when he came to the place and saw him, passed by on the other side. But a Samaritan, as he journeyed, came to where he was, and when he saw him, he had compassion. He went to him and bound up his wounds, pouring on oil and wine. Then he set him on his own animal and brought him to an inn and took care of him. And the next day he took out two denarii and gave them to the innkeeper, saying, 'Take care of him, and whatever more you spend, I will repay you when I come back.' Which of these three, do you think, proved to be a neighbor to the man who fell among the robbers?" He said, "The one who showed him mercy." And Jesus said to him, "You go, and do likewise." (Luke 10:25–37)

Either Jesus was living in fantasy, was a liar or worse, or otherwise He is exactly who He said He was, God in the flesh.

We first observe that the person asking the question was likely not a lawyer as we think of one today. He was literally an "expert in the law" in the original Greek. The Jews at that time referred to someone as an expert in the law if he was a Bible scholar, someone who was an expert in the first five books of the Bible, commonly called "the law" by the Jews of that time. Such a person would probably be called a "Bible scholar" today. For that reason, we will refer to the lawyer in this account as the *Bible scholar* or just the *scholar*.

One intriguing feature of this parable is that it answers two questions at the same time. The first is, "'Teacher, what I must I do to inherit eternal life?'" And the second is, "'And who is my neighbor?'" By their very nature, parables are directed to only one theme or lesson, not two. Any parable that answers two questions at once is an unusually sophisticated parable. As we will see, the way Jesus answered these questions is even more brilliant.

A useful way of explaining this parable is to point out that Jesus answered the two questions by constructing a parable with three levels of meaning.

1. *The first level of meaning answers the question "Who is my neighbor?"* The Jews generally believed that they could ignore the needs of Gentiles, and they could certainly disregard the needs of Samaritans, whom they detested. (When asked, "Who was neighbor to the man who fell among the robbers?" the Bible scholar couldn't even bring himself to speak the word *Samaritan*. He referred to him only as "the one who showed him mercy.") We notice, however, that it is the Samaritan who was a neighbor to the man who fell into the hands of thieves, while the priest and Levite—both Jews— did not. So Jesus answered the question in a manner that was both indirect and powerful: The parable illustrates the moral standard that to inherit eternal life we must, as stated by the expert in the law, "love our neighbors as ourselves." But what he did not say is that we must recognize that everyone is our neighbor.

    Since many people are familiar with this parable, we could ask them what they believe it means. They might answer along the lines of saying that we should love our neighbor by helping those in need. That answer is correct, but there are also two more levels of meaning in the parable. Even many Bible commentaries fail to get beyond this first level. Some, however, explain the three levels of meaning very well.[41] This means that Jesus, the master teacher, was even more sophisticated in His teaching than many of the well-educated and gifted Bible scholars who have tried to explain what He said.

2. *The second level of meaning involves the way the Bible scholar should*

---

41   Matthew Henry understood the parable very well. His commentary on Luke can be accessed online at www.ccel.org/ccel/henry/mhc5.Luke.i.html.

have personally related to the story. With whom would he have identified? It would not have been the Samaritan, as the Bible scholar refused to even speak the word *Samaritan.* The two travelers who looked the other way, however, were Jews like the Bible scholar himself. Additionally, they were Jews of high standing like him. The scholar would have easily identified with the two Jews and thereby should have been reminded of the many people in need to whom he had personally turned a blind eye and a deaf ear. So, the second level of meaning logically follows from what we have here observed: *To inherit eternal life, you must love your neighbor as yourself—which you have not done.*

In His parable, Jesus was indirectly but effectively showing the scholar that he was a sinner. Jesus spoke to him, not of the evil he had done, but of the good he had not done. The parable reminds us of a conversation Jesus had with another Jewish man. There, Jesus said that to receive eternal life you must "love your neighbor as yourself" (Matthew 19:19). That young man replied by saying: "All these [moral laws] I have kept" (19:20). In that conversation, also, Jesus indirectly demonstrated to the man that he was failing to keep the moral law. The Bible scholar was likely of the same mind. Jesus was showing him that he could not be saved by keeping the moral law because he, in fact, had not kept it. Jesus was showing him his need for a Savior.

3. *The third level of meaning requires us to identify the Samaritan.* Who was this man? An outcast in the eyes of the Jewish leaders? A man who went out of his way to help those in need? Someone who wrote a blank check for another man's healing, saying, "Whatever more you spend, I will repay you when I come back"? This Samaritan was willing to pay any price. He also said he was coming back—to settle up any and all accounts. The Samaritan symbolizes Jesus, the Savior of the world, the God-man, who came to seek and to save those who are lost, including this scholar.

The third level of meaning is this: To inherit eternal life you must look to the Messiah of God, who has come to live and die so that your sins, your moral failures, will be forgiven. You must put your trust in the one who will rise again from the grave to demonstrate that the price for your salvation has been paid in full and to show that this wondrous message is sure and true. *The third level of meaning, and by far the most important, is the Gospel message of* salvation through Jesus Christ. John Newton described this all-important truth in his hymn "How Kind the Good Samaritan," which begins as follows:

> How kind the good Samaritan
> To him who fell among the thieves!
> Thus Jesus pities fallen man,
> And heals the wounds the soul receives.[42]

This is the primary meaning of the parable. It is directed to the first and most important question of the scholar, "What shall I do to inherit eternal life?" (Luke 10:25). The answer is in the man telling the story: Jesus, the master teacher who gave indirect and brilliant answers to both questions posed by the Bible scholar. He is no fool. He is no impostor. He is no charlatan. He can only be the person He claimed to be and that Luke and the other Gospel writers said He is—the promised Messiah and Lord of all. In His teaching, Jesus always pointed His listeners to Himself and what He came on earth to do. This parable is no exception. This parable embodies the reason why Jesus the Nazarene has had such a profound impact on human history.

We may wonder why Jesus was so indirect in this parable. In answer, Jesus was often indirect in His teaching. That may be in part because His audience was often hostile to what He said. This was likely the case here. The questions of the Bible scholar were something less than straightforward. Luke tells us the questions were asked to "test Jesus," not because the scholar was looking for answers. Insincere questions often require indirect answers. Yet, Jesus answered the questions even though they were disingenuous. They gave Him the opportunity to proclaim both the moral law and the glorious Gospel message that the Messiah had come and stood before them. The power to save lost souls is in the Gospel message alone.

> The power to save lost souls is in the Gospel message alone.

JESUS' TEACHING ON DIVORCE

There are many other examples that can be given to illustrate the masterful way that Jesus taught. One such example that was also referenced in a previous context is recorded in Matthew 19:

> And Pharisees came up to Him and tested Him by asking, "Is it lawful to divorce one's wife for any cause?" He answered, "Have you not read that He who created them from the beginning made

---

42 Newton, *Olney*.

them male and female, and said, 'Therefore a man shall leave his father and his mother and hold fast to his wife, and the two shall become one flesh'? So they are no longer two but one flesh. What therefore God has joined together, let not man separate." They said to Him, "Why then did Moses command one to give a certificate of divorce and to send her away?" He said to them, "Because of your hardness of heart Moses allowed you to divorce your wives, but from the beginning it was not so. And I say to you: whoever divorces his wife, except for sexual immorality, and marries another, commits adultery." (vv. 3–9)

The Pharisees here confronted Jesus with a dilemma. They believed that if, on the one hand, as noted above, He said that divorce without cause was wrong, He would be contradicting Moses and would thereby be violating a major criterion for true prophets of God. If, on the other hand, He said that divorce without cause was acceptable, He would then be contradicting His own teaching on marriage and divorce.[43] Either way, the Pharisees thought that they had put Jesus in a no-win situation. They thought Jesus was on the horns of a dilemma.

Jesus, however, easily escaped their trap, saying, "Because of your hardness of heart Moses allowed you to divorce your wives, but from the beginning it was not so. And I say to you: whoever divorces his wife, except for sexual immorality, and marries another, commits adultery" (v. 9). In this way, Jesus demonstrated His superior understanding of the Law of Moses compared to that of the Pharisees, even though many of the Pharisees were recognized scholars on the books of Moses. Some of these experts even memorized the five books of Moses verbatim. As can be seen, however, a person having memorized something doesn't necessarily mean that it is understood.

In addition, Jesus revealed that He understood the nature of civil law as stated by Moses better than the Pharisees. Jesus understood that civil law can go only so far in prohibiting immoral acts. Modern lawmakers know this; the Pharisees apparently did not, or at least they were unwilling to admit that they did. Once again, Jesus displayed the highest level of sophistication in His teaching. As always, He put the experts, the scholars, to shame.

> Jesus displayed the highest level of sophistication in His teaching. As always, He put the experts, the scholars, to shame.

---

43 See Matthew 5:31–32. Jesus was speaking of the moral law, not the civil law, when He said that divorce without cause was wrong. Moses, in allowing divorce, was speaking of the civil law.

JESUS' TEACHING ABOUT HEALING ON THE SABBATH

Another example of Jesus' superior understanding of the nature of civil law, and hence His superior teaching, is recorded in Matthew 12:

> He went on from there and entered their synagogue. And a man was there with a withered hand. And they asked Him, "Is it lawful to heal on the Sabbath?"—so that they might accuse Him. He said to them, "Which one of you who has a sheep, if it falls into a pit on the Sabbath, will not take hold of it and lift it out? Of how much more value is a man than a sheep! So it is lawful to do good on the Sabbath." Then He said to the man, "Stretch out your hand." And the man stretched it out, and it was restored, healthy like the other. But the Pharisees went out and conspired against Him, how to destroy Him. (vv. 9–14)

In looking at this exchange, we should first note that the laws given by Moses did not forbid miraculous healing on the Sabbath. The Mosaic Law prohibited work on the Sabbath; it was the Jewish leaders who wrongly defined miraculous healing as work. That means that we are not dealing with God's ceremonial or moral law in this debate; we are instead dealing with the rules and regulations of men.[44]

We will see in chapter 14 that acts of charity as described here by Jesus follow the highest level of moral reasoning, while the analysis of the Pharisees was based on low-level reasoning, that of legalism. On the issues of breaking the Sabbath, the debates always took this form. Not surprisingly, Jesus consistently came out on top. The Jewish leaders usually seemed to sense that they had lost the debate, but they never appeared to be able to figure out why. The reason they lost was because Jesus understood the moral law far better than they did. So these Jewish leaders decided that since they couldn't defeat Jesus in debate, they would kill Him instead. Once again, we see Jesus as the master teacher—and in this case, the master of debate who displayed a masterful understanding of the issues at hand.

In all these examples, we see Jesus as the master teacher. He created a parable with three levels of meaning. He displayed an in-depth and accurate understanding of moral reasoning and the moral law. He revealed a precise

---

44 To illustrate this, we look at the role of the courts in the United States. A court must often define a term in the Constitution, just as the Jewish leaders defined terms in the Mosaic Law. At times, however, when terms are defined to the minute detail, the definition can become inaccurate and the term misused. This was the case with the Jewish leaders and their attempt to define *work*.

and sophisticated understanding of the writings of Moses, and He won arguments by being skilled at logical argumentation and by knowing what was true and what was false. Was this man a charlatan? Was He mentally ill? Was He a fool? Not a chance. The standard of consistency makes such views impossible. As C. S. Lewis pointed out above, if Jesus was a master teacher, He must have also been much more than that. Jesus claimed to be God in the flesh. That claim leaves us with two options: either He was a liar, a lunatic, or worse; or He was exactly who He said He was—the Son of the living God. There are no other options. The criterion of consistency as well as the previously stated standards for true prophets requires this conclusion. We do well to take Him very seriously.

QUESTIONS FOR REVIEW AND DISCUSSION

1. We have seen from statements by C. S. Lewis that he, too, was a masterful teacher. Yet he did not generate the kind of opposition that Jesus did. How might we account for this difference?

2. What would you say are some of the qualities of good teachers? Do these qualities fit Jesus of Nazareth? Why or why not?

CHAPTER 6

MIRACLES

When the disciples of John the Baptist came to Jesus and asked Him if He was the promised Messiah, Jesus replied,

> Go and tell John what you have seen and heard: the blind receive their sight, the lame walk, lepers are cleansed, and the deaf hear, the dead are raised up, the poor have good news preached to them. And blessed is the one who is not offended by Me. (Luke 7:22–23)

With these words, Jesus instructed John's followers to tell him that Jesus was performing extraordinary miracles that clearly demonstrated that He was a true prophet of God. As we will see, the miracles that would be reported to John additionally revealed that Jesus was not just a true prophet of God, but the promised Messiah of God. We will come to understand that Jesus' miracles, which far exceeded the miracles of the Old Testament prophets, could only be accomplished by God Himself. We will see that while the miracles of the Old Testament prophets demonstrated that the Lord God was working through them, Jesus' miracles pointed directly to Himself as God. We will also see that we have good reason to recognize that the miracles are genuine events of history.

JESUS HEALS THE BLIND MAN

We begin with John 9:

> As He [Jesus] passed by, He saw a man blind from birth. And His disciples asked Him, "Rabbi, who sinned, this man or his parents, that he was born blind?" Jesus answered, "It was not that this man sinned, or his parents, but that the works of God might be displayed in him. We must work the works of Him who sent Me while it is day; night is coming, when no one can work. As long as

I am in the world, I am the light of the world." Having said these things, He spit on the ground and made mud with the saliva. Then He anointed the man's eyes with the mud and said to him, "Go, wash in the pool of Siloam" (which means Sent). So he went and washed and came back seeing.

The neighbors and those who had seen him before as a beggar were saying, "Is this not the man who used to sit and beg?" Some said, "It is he." Others said, "No, but he is like him." He kept saying, "I am the man." So they said to him, "Then how were your eyes opened?" He answered, "The man called Jesus made mud and anointed my eyes and said to me, 'Go to Siloam and wash.' So I went and washed and received my sight." They said to him, "Where is He?" He said, "I do not know."

They brought to the Pharisees the man who had formerly been blind. Now it was a Sabbath day when Jesus made the mud and opened his eyes. So the Pharisees again asked him how he had received his sight. And he said to them, "He put mud on my eyes, and I washed, and I see." Some of the Pharisees said, "This man is not from God, for He does not keep the Sabbath." But others said, "How can a man who is a sinner do such signs?" And there was a division among them. So they said again to the blind man, "What do you say about Him, since He has opened your eyes?" He said, "He is a prophet."

The Jews did not believe that he had been blind and had received his sight, until they called the parents of the man who had received his sight and asked them, "Is this your son, who you say was born blind? How then does he now see?" His parents answered, "We know that this is our son and that he was born blind. But how he now sees we do not know, nor do we know who opened his eyes. Ask him; he is of age. He will speak for himself." (His parents said these things because they feared the Jews, for the Jews had already agreed that if anyone should confess Jesus to be Christ, he was to be put out of the synagogue.) Therefore his parents said, "He is of age; ask him."

So for the second time they called the man who had been blind and said to him, "Give glory to God. We know that this man [Jesus] is a sinner." He answered, "Whether He is a sinner I do not know. One thing I do know, that though I was blind, now I see."

They said to him, "What did He do to you? How did He open your eyes?" He answered them, "I have told you already, and you would not listen. Why do you want to hear it again? Do you also want to become His disciples?" And they reviled him, saying, "You are His disciple, but we are disciples of Moses. We know that God has spoken to Moses, but as for this man, we do not know where He comes from." The man answered, "Why, this is an amazing thing! You do not know where He comes from, and yet He opened my eyes. We know that God does not listen to sinners, but if anyone is a worshiper of God and does His will, God listens to him. Never since the world began has it been heard that anyone opened the eyes of a man born blind. If this man were not from God, He could do nothing." They answered him, "You were born in utter sin, and would you teach us?" And they cast him out.

Jesus heard that they had cast him out, and having found him He said, "Do you believe in the Son of Man?" He answered, "And who is He, sir, that I may believe in Him?" Jesus said to him, "You have seen Him, and it is He who is speaking to you." He said, "Lord, I believe," and he worshiped Him. (vv. 1–38)

There are numerous points of interest in this account. One is described by the man healed of his blindness as he said: "Never since the world began has it been heard that anyone opened the eyes of a man born blind" (v. 32). Even though the prophets who preceded Jesus had performed sensational miracles, there were no accounts of them ever healing someone who had been blind since birth. Doing so may have required the creation of new biological structures of some kind that would allow this man to see.[45] Even today, there is no medical cure for infants born blind.

Up until this time, the Jewish authorities had been attempting to explain Jesus' miracles by saying He performed them by Satan's power. That was not an option here. This miracle was too great, too sensational, to attribute to Satan. It had never been done before. Their standard explanation for the miracles of Jesus was now in ruins. They simply had to find another excuse. So they called in the man's parents, hoping that the man who could now see was someone other than their son who had been born blind. To their dismay,

---

45 According to the Texas School for the Blind and Visually Impaired (www.tsbvi.edu/seehear/spring99/opticnerve.htm), optic nerve hypoplasia (ONH), the underdevelopment of the optic nerve during pregnancy, is one of the top three most common causes of visual impairment in children. It can occur in one eye but most commonly it takes place in both. ONH cannot be cured.

the parents said: "We know that this is our son and that he was born blind" (v. 20).

We also see the significance in what Jesus said just before He healed the man: "I am the light of the world" (v. 5). That statement is a clear reference to Genesis 1:3, where God said, "Let there be light." Only God can create light, so Jesus was identifying Himself as God the Creator. John had introduced Him to us that way when he said, "All things were made through Him" (John 1:3), and "In Him was life, and the life was the light of men" (1:4). In this miracle, Jesus identified Himself not only as a prophet but also as God in the flesh. We remember that the miracles of the prophets always pointed to the Lord God; Jesus' miracles always pointed to Himself.

Finding no escape, and in their desperation, the Jewish leaders called in the man who had been healed for a second time and accosted him, saying: "You are His disciple, but we are disciples of Moses. We know that God has spoken to Moses, but as for this man, we do not know where He comes from" (9:28–29). The man, however, was not in the least bit intimidated, and replied to the accusations against him by calmly stating the obvious: "Never since the world began has it been heard that anyone opened the eyes of a man born blind. If this man were not from God, He could do nothing" (vv. 32–33).

Jesus' enemies now recognized that there was no escaping the significance of this miracle. It was proof positive that Jesus really was the Messiah. As a consequence, they gave up their inquisition, and in total frustration and anger, they cast the man out from their presence.

We should observe here that overwhelming evidence is not enough to bring people into the kingdom of God. These Jewish leaders had conclusive evidence. The rational response would have been for them to admit that Jesus had performed a sensational miracle, a miracle that only God Himself could do. But admitting as much meant they would have to recognize Jesus as the Messiah of God. This they refused to do. As is sometimes said, "The same sun that melts the ice, hardens the clay." No amount of evidence will convince those who refuse to believe.

The same is true in our day regarding the resurrection of Jesus. It appears you cannot recognize that the resurrection actually happened in history without also acknowledging Jesus as the Messiah of God, the Creator and Ruler of all things. You can't do so without falling on your knees and saying, "My Lord and my God!" The evidence is there, but many people simply refuse to believe.

We should also observe that this narrative describing how Jesus' enemies tried to escape the implications of His healing the man born blind clearly has the ring of truth about it. The same can be said for every narrative in the Gospel accounts. Just by reading the accounts, their truth becomes evident. These records consistently mirror the manner in which people actually behave, and they give a historical narrative that is remarkably consistent throughout. The Gospel accounts really do speak for themselves. And as we have observed, the power of God to salvation is in the Good News of Jesus Christ as proclaimed in the Gospels. (See chapter 9 for more information on the reliability of the New Testament accounts.)

JESUS RAISES LAZARUS FROM THE DEAD

Another of Jesus' sensational miracles is recorded in John 11:

> Then Jesus, deeply moved again, came to the tomb. It was a cave, and a stone lay against it. Jesus said, "Take away the stone." Martha, the sister of the dead man, said to Him, "Lord, by this time there will be an odor, for he has been dead four days." Jesus said to her, "Did I not tell you that if you believed you would see the glory of God?" So they took away the stone. And Jesus lifted up His eyes and said, "Father, I thank You that You have heard Me. I knew that You always hear Me, but I said this on account of the people standing around, that they may believe that You sent Me." When He had said these things, He cried out with a loud voice, "Lazarus, come out." The man who had died came out, his hands and feet bound with linen strips, and his face wrapped with a cloth. Jesus said to them, "Unbind him, and let him go."
>
> Many of the Jews therefore, who had come with Mary and had seen what He did, believed in Him, but some of them went to the Pharisees and told them what Jesus had done. So the chief priests and the Pharisees gathered the council and said, "What are we to do? For this man performs many signs. If we let Him go on like this, everyone will believe in Him, and the Romans will come and take away both our place and our nation." But one of them, Caiaphas, who was high priest that year, said to them, "You know nothing at all. Nor do you understand that it is better for you that one man should die for the people, not that the whole nation should perish." He did not say this of his own accord, but being high priest that year he prophesied that Jesus would die for the nation, and not for the nation only, but also to gather into one the children of God who are scattered abroad. So from that day on they made plans to put Him to death. (vv. 38–53)

Here, we see another miracle that goes way beyond the miracles of the Old Testament. The prophet Elijah had raised the widow's son from the dead (1 Kings 17:17-24), and Elisha raised the Shunammite's son from the dead (2 Kings 4:32-36), but in both cases the boys had only been dead a short time. Lazarus had been dead for four days. Even Martha, Jesus' devoted follower, was skeptical. She said, "Lord, by this time there will be an odor, for he has been dead four days" (John 11:39). Martha knew that after four days, the body would have been partly decomposed. No prophet had ever raised a body in that condition back to life. No one could do such a thing—no one, that is, but God Himself.

If Jesus had authority over the body and life of Lazarus, would He not have authority over all life? Peter told the people gathered at Solomon's Colonnade: "You killed the Author of life" (Acts 3:15). As such, we are reminded this is the same Jesus who created life, the same Jesus who created the heavens and the earth by the power of His word. As noted above, John explained all this as he began his Gospel by saying: "In the beginning was the Word, and the Word was with God, and the Word was God. He was in the beginning with God. All things were made through Him, and without Him was not any thing made that was made" (John 1:1-3). The raising of Lazarus is a microcosm of one of Jesus' greatest miracles, the creation of the universe as described above by John. No miracle recorded in the Old Testament revealed a prophet to be the "Author of life." This miracle of Jesus raising Lazarus from the dead not only identified Jesus as a true prophet but also once again established Him as the Creator God Himself.

As we have seen before, many of the Jews put their faith in Jesus because of what He had done. Many others did not. Once again, Jesus' enemies knew the extraordinary significance of what He had done. They lamented: "If we let Him go on like this, everyone will believe in Him, and the Romans will come and take away both our place and our nation" (11:48). (The second half of the Jews' statement is false. Jesus was no threat to the safety of the Jewish nation, but reasoning based on false premises was typical of the Jewish leaders.)

Once again, Jesus' enemies were totally irrational in their response. By force of the evidence, they should have concluded that Jesus really was who He said He was. In addition, they should have foreseen that just as Lazarus had been raised from the dead, Jesus could be raised from the dead as well. In this case, killing Him would be the ultimate folly. But these leaders couldn't see that, and as a consequence, they became tools of the living God to carry out the sacrifice of the Paschal Lamb for the salvation of all people.

The raising of Lazarus was so sensational that news of it spread quickly. This explains the king's welcome the crowd gave Jesus shortly thereafter on Palm Sunday. John describes this event in chapter 12, saying, "The crowd that had been with Him when He called Lazarus out of the tomb and raised him from the dead continued to bear witness. The reason why the crowd went to meet Him was that they heard He had done this sign" (vv. 17–18).

HISTORICAL ACCOUNTS OF JESUS' MIRACLES

There are many other miracles of Jesus we could bring up here, but we shall instead turn to the fact that we even have non-Christian accounts of Jesus' miracles. The Jewish historian Flavius Josephus (AD 37–100) said, "Now there was about this time Jesus, a wise man, if it be lawful to call him a man, for he was a doer of wonderful works, a teacher of such men as receive the truth with pleasure."[46]

As we can see, Josephus testified that Jesus "was a doer of wonderful works" (sensational miracles). Because Josephus was a very early historian, he would have had access to many of the people who were contemporaries of Jesus and who could have given firsthand testimony about His life. We also note that Josephus was commissioned by the Roman government to write the history of the Jews. As a result, he would have had access to all the official records surrounding Jesus' life and death. In addition, Josephus was not sympathetic to Jesus and His followers. He had no reason to slant his writing in a way that would have been favorable to Christianity. There was no historian with better credentials than Josephus when it came to the history of the Jews at the time of Jesus, the Christ.

In addition to Josephus, the Jewish Talmud (Jewish religious writings) of that time also acknowledged that Jesus performed miracles. A statement in the Jewish Talmud written not much later than AD 100 states that at the time of the Passover, Jesus of Nazareth was executed by crucifixion for the crime of sorcery.[47] As we know, Jesus' enemies acknowledged His miracles but claimed He did them by Satan's power. That would make His miracles sorcery as the Jewish leaders interpreted them.

For Jesus' enemies to admit to His miracles is especially powerful testimony. In a court of law, testimony like this would have a high level of credibility because it came from what attorneys call a hostile witness, someone who would much prefer that what he was saying was not true. Such testimony is of great importance because it reveals that even Jesus' enemies

---

46 Josephus, *Works of Josephus*, 379.
47 *Babylonian Talmud*.

admitted that He performed miracles. There was no doubt as to His miracles; the only question was the power behind them. We also take note of the many examples in the four Gospels of the Jewish leaders criticizing Jesus for healing on the Sabbath. These leaders knew that performing miracles was one of the tests of true prophets, and they couldn't deny Jesus' miracles, so they instead attacked Him for supposedly violating the Sabbath, part of the moral code given by Moses. Disagreeing with Moses was a mark of false prophets. Jesus, however, was not violating what Moses had said; He was disagreeing with the Jewish leaders' faulty interpretation of Mosaic Law. These Jewish leaders, as we have seen, were legalists in the way they understood and applied the Law of Moses; but Jesus understood the Mosaic law much better than they did.

At the time, Jesus' miracles were common knowledge among the people living in and around Jerusalem, as Peter indicated in his speech at Pentecost when he said: "Men of Israel, hear these words: Jesus of Nazareth, a man attested to you by God with mighty works and wonders and signs that God did through Him in your midst, as you yourselves know" (Acts 2:22). Paul similarly appealed to the many secular reports of Jesus' miracles when he said to King Agrippa: "For the king knows about these things, and to him I speak boldly. For I am persuaded that none of these things has escaped his notice, for this has not been done in a corner" (Acts 26:26).

As we know, some church leaders of our time also deny that Jesus performed such miracles. Miracles just don't happen, they often say. The miracles and the historical narrative, however, mesh together perfectly. You can't take the miracles out and have anything left. Jesus' enemies couldn't bring themselves to really accept the miracles either, even though they could not deny them. They couldn't accept the miracles because they refused to accept the implications. The same is true today. But refusing to accept the truth and the significance of Jesus' miracles puts a person in great peril. Jesus described the danger in this response:

> Then He began to denounce the cities where most of His mighty works had been done, because they did not repent. "Woe to you, Chorazin! Woe to you, Bethsaida! For if the mighty works done in you had been done in Tyre and Sidon, they would have repented long ago in sackcloth and ashes. But I tell you, it will be more bearable on the day of judgment for Tyre and Sidon than for you. And you, Capernaum, will you be exalted to heaven? You will be brought down to Hades. For if the mighty works done in you had

been done in Sodom, it would have remained until this day. But I tell you that it will be more tolerable on the day of judgment for the land of Sodom than for you." (Matthew 11:20–24)

Resisting the testimony of the Holy Spirit regarding Jesus' miracles is done at great risk.

> Resisting the testimony of the Holy Spirit regarding Jesus' miracles is done at great risk.

The miracles of Jesus are well-documented truths of history. There is objective and verifiable evidence that Jesus actually performed these miracles. Jesus did these miracles in genuine history as attested to by a number of credible historical documents. His miracles didn't simply establish Jesus as a true prophet; the extraordinary *magnitude* of His miracles established Him as God in the flesh—the Creator God of heaven and earth. And we remember that just because certain writings are included in the Bible, that doesn't in any way reduce their value as historical documents. Christianity is based on history. The only reason for denying these miracles of Jesus is a preconceived prejudice that they did not, or could not, happen.

QUESTIONS FOR REVIEW AND DISCUSSION

1. It is not unusual for people to say, "I don't believe in miracles, the reason being that I've never seen one." How might you respond to someone with that viewpoint?

2. Some people say, "We don't even know if there ever was a Jesus of Nazareth." Is that a reasonable statement? How might you respond to someone who says this?

CHAPTER 7

FULFILLMENT OF PROPHECY

Luke personally accompanied Paul on several missionary journeys. While on the final journey, he recorded Paul's speech to King Agrippa and his court. The speech was Paul's opportunity to defend himself against the vague charges the Jewish leaders had brought against him, but he used it to deliver a missionary sermon instead. In that presentation, Paul said,

> "King Agrippa, do you believe the prophets? I know that you believe." And Agrippa said to Paul, "In a short time would you persuade me to be a Christian?" And Paul said, "Whether short or long, I would to God that not only you but also all who hear me this day might become such as I am—except for these chains." (Acts 26:27-29)

Paul knew that Agrippa was familiar with the beliefs and customs of the Jews. That enabled Paul to indirectly tell Agrippa that Jesus' fulfillment of the Old Testament messianic prophecies provides powerful evidence that Jesus truly is the Messiah, the Son of the living God. In this way, Paul implied to Agrippa that he, too, should become a believer, and Agrippa made it clear that he understood exactly what Paul was saying.

The Old Testament revolves around the prophecies of the coming Messiah. Jesus' coming is the theme, the unifying thread, of the entire Old Testament narrative. These messianic prophecies began immediately after the fall into sin. As God spoke to the serpent, He made this promise: "I will put enmity between you and the woman, and between your offspring and her offspring [in Hebrew, seed]; He shall bruise your head, and you shall bruise His heel" (Genesis 3:15).

> Jesus' coming is the theme, the unifying thread, of the entire Old Testament narrative.

God promised He would send someone who would be the "seed of the woman," a human being descended from

Eve, who would set things right again by bruising the head of the serpent. It is not surprising, then, that Luke traced the genealogy of Jesus all the way back to Adam and Eve. He did so to show that Jesus was the Seed of the woman who had been promised to Adam and Eve in the garden.

This same promise was restated to Abraham centuries after Adam and Eve. God said to Abraham: "And in your offspring [seed] shall all the nations of the earth be blessed" (Genesis 22:18). Here, God narrowed down the genetic history of the Messiah considerably. The seed of Eve would include all persons who would ever live. By means of God's promise to Abraham, we see that the Messiah could come from his descendants only.

The apostle Paul specifically clarified that Jesus is the fulfillment of this promise made to Abraham: "Now the promises were made to Abraham and to his offspring. It does not say, 'And to offsprings,' referring to many, but referring to one, 'And to your offspring,' who is Christ" (Galatians 3:16).

Notice that Paul referred to God's "promises," plural. What are these promises? God had also promised Abraham that he would be the father of a great nation. That promise is recorded in Genesis 17:4–8:

> Behold, My covenant is with you, and you shall be the father of a multitude of nations. No longer shall your name be called Abram, but your name shall be Abraham, for I have made you the father of a multitude of nations. I will make you exceedingly fruitful, and I will make you into nations, and kings shall come from you. And I will establish My covenant between Me and you and your offspring after you throughout their generations for an everlasting covenant, to be God to you and to your offspring after you. And I will give to you and to your offspring after you the land of your sojournings, all the land of Canaan, for an everlasting possession, and I will be their God.

Here, we see that God made a covenant with Abraham, a covenant with the promise that not only would the promised Messiah be born from his offspring, but that God would make Abraham's descendants into a great nation as well. In addition, God promised Abraham that the land of Canaan, a land "flowing in milk and honey" (Exodus 3:8), would be the possession of his descendants until the end of time.

The genetic line of the Messiah was narrowed again when God told Abraham this chosen nation that would give rise to the Messiah would come through Isaac, not Ishmael. God said to Abraham: "Be not displeased because of the boy and because of your slave woman. Whatever Sarah says to you, do as she tells you, for through Isaac shall your offspring be named" (Genesis 21:12).

The line of descent of the Messiah was narrowed again when Isaac's son Jacob was identified to carry on the line of descent. Numbers 24:17–19 reads as follows:

> A star shall come out of Jacob,
>   and a scepter shall rise out of Israel;
> it shall crush the forehead of Moab
>   and break down all the sons of Sheth.
> Edom shall be dispossessed;
>   Seir also, his enemies, shall be dispossessed.
> Israel is doing valiantly.
> And one from Jacob shall exercise dominion
>   and destroy the survivors of cities!

Jacob had twelve sons. Which son would carry on the line of descent of the Messiah? Genesis 49:10 answers that question as it says, "The scepter shall not depart from Judah, nor the ruler's staff from between his feet, until tribute comes to him; and to Him shall be the obedience of the peoples."

We now fast-forward to the time of King David and his father, Jesse. Isaiah prophesied this:

> There shall come forth a shoot from the stump of Jesse,
>   and a branch from his roots shall bear fruit.
> And the Spirit of the Lord shall rest upon Him,
>   the Spirit of wisdom and understanding,
>   the Spirit of counsel and might,
>   the Spirit of knowledge and the fear of the Lord.
> And His delight shall be in the fear of the Lord.
> He shall not judge by what His eyes see,
>   or decide disputes by what His ears hear,
> but with righteousness He shall judge the poor,
>   and decide with equity for the meek of the earth;
> and He shall strike the earth with the rod of His mouth,
>   and with the breath of His lips He shall kill the wicked.
> Righteousness shall be the belt of His waist,
>   and faithfulness the belt of His loins.
> The wolf shall dwell with the lamb,
>   and the leopard shall lie down with the young goat,
>   and the calf and the lion and the fattened calf together;
>   and a little child shall lead them. . . .

> In that day the root of Jesse, who shall stand as a signal for the peoples—of Him shall the nations inquire, and His resting place shall be glorious. (Isaiah 11:1–6, 10)

Jesse had eight sons, but it was David, the youngest, who was chosen not only to be king but also to be in the line of descent to the Messiah. Jeremiah said,

> Behold, the days are coming, declares the LORD, when I will raise up for David a righteous Branch, and He shall reign as king and deal wisely, and shall execute justice and righteousness in the land. In His days Judah will be saved, and Israel will dwell securely. And this is the name by which He will be called: "The LORD is our righteousness." (23:5–6)

The Gospels include numerous occasions where Jesus was called "the son of David." Each of these references point to the fulfillment of the prophecy and the promise that the Messiah would be a descendant of David. Beginning with David, the prophets began to give us numerous specific details about the coming Messiah. David, for instance, prophesied that the Messiah would be killed and then rise from the dead. David wrote:

> I have set the LORD always before me;
>   because He is at my right hand, I shall not be shaken.
> Therefore my heart is glad, and my whole being rejoices;
>   my flesh also dwells secure.
> For You will not abandon my soul to Sheol,
>   or let Your holy one see corruption
> You make known to me the path of life;
>   in Your presence there is fullness of joy;
>   at Your right hand are pleasures forevermore.
> (Psalm 16:8–11)

In these words, David was not speaking about himself. He was prophesying that the Messiah, though killed, would not decompose in the grave (not be abandoned nor "see corruption") but would be raised to life ("You make known to me the path of life"). As we saw in chapter 2 of this book, Peter explained to the crowd at Pentecost that Jesus fulfilled this prophecy:

> Being therefore a prophet, and knowing that God had sworn with an oath to him that He would set one of his descendants on his throne, he foresaw and spoke about the resurrection of the Christ, that He was not abandoned to Hades, nor did His flesh see

corruption. This Jesus God raised up, and of that we all are witnesses. (Acts 2:30–32)

David also prophesied that the Messiah would be killed by crucifixion—even though, in David's time, this barbaric means of execution was unknown. In Psalm 22, David said,

> My God, my God, why have You forsaken Me?
>> Why are You so far from saving Me, from the words of My groaning?
> O my God, I cry by day, but You do not answer,
>> and by night, but I find no rest.
> Yet You are holy,
>> enthroned on the praises of Israel.
> In You our fathers trusted;
>> they trusted, and You delivered them.
> To You they cried and were rescued;
>> in You they trusted and were not put to shame.
> But I am a worm and not a man,
>> scorned by mankind and despised by the people.
> All who see Me mock Me;
>> they make mouths at Me; they wag their heads;
> "He trusts in the LORD; let Him deliver Him;
>> let Him rescue Him, for He delights in Him!"
> Yet You are He who took Me from the womb;
>> You made me trust You at My mother's breasts.
> On You was I cast from My birth,
>> and from My mother's womb You have been My God.
> Be not far from Me,
>> for trouble is near,
>> and there is none to help.
> Many bulls encompass Me;
>> strong bulls of Bashan surround Me;
> they open wide their mouths at Me,
>> like a ravening and roaring lion.
> I am poured out like water,
>> and all My bones are out of joint;
> My heart is like wax;
>> it is melted within My breast;

> My strength is dried up like a potsherd,
>   and My tongue sticks to My jaws;
>   you lay Me in the dust of death.
>
> For dogs encompass Me;
>   a company of evildoers encircles Me;
>   they have pierced My hands and feet—
> I can count all my bones—
>   they stare and gloat over Me;
>   they divide My garments among them,
>   and for My clothing they cast lots. (vv. 1–18)

This is an unmistakable description of Jesus on the cross. The apostle John specifically pointed out how the crucifixion of Jesus fulfilled the last two lines of this prophecy:

> When the soldiers had crucified Jesus, they took His garments and divided them into four parts, one part for each soldier; also His tunic. But the tunic was seamless, woven in one piece from top to bottom, so they said to one another, "Let us not tear it, but cast lots for it to see whose it shall be." This was to fulfill the Scripture which says,
>
> > "They divided My garments among them,
> >   and for My clothing they cast lots." (John 19:23–24)

Jesus' fulfillment of specific messianic prophecies like these make it crystal clear the He is the promised Messiah of God. Additionally, Jesus' fulfillment of such prophecies gave further confirmation that prophets who were recognized as authentic were actually true prophets of God.

There are many other messianic prophecies that Jesus fulfilled, prophecies that further established Him as the promised Messiah. Following are some of them:

The Messiah would be God Himself.

Prophecy: "For to us a child is born, to us a son is given; and the government shall be upon His shoulders, and His name shall be called Wonderful Counselor, Mighty God, Everlasting Father, Prince of Peace" (Isaiah 9:6).

Fulfillment: "In the beginning was the Word [Jesus], and the Word was with God, and the Word was God" (John 1:1; see also vv. 9–16).

The Messiah would be born in Bethlehem.
  Prophecy: "But you, O Bethlehem Ephrathah, who are too little to be among the clans of Judah, from you shall come forth for Me one who is to be ruler in Israel, whose coming forth is from of old, from ancient days" (Micah 5:2).
  Fulfillment: "And the angel said to her, 'Do not be afraid, Mary, for you have found favor with God. And behold, you will conceive in your womb and bear a son, and you shall call His name Jesus. He will be great and will be called the Son of the Most High. And the Lord God will give to Him the throne of His father David, and He will reign over the house of Jacob forever, and of His kingdom there will be no end.'
  "And Mary said to the angel, 'How will this be, since I am a virgin?'
  "And the angel answered her, 'The Holy Spirit will come upon you, and the power of the Most High will overshadow you; therefore the child to be born will be called holy—the Son of God'" (Luke 1:30–35).

The Messiah would be born of a virgin.
  Prophecy: "Therefore the Lord Himself will give you a sign. Behold, the virgin shall conceive and bear a son, and shall call His name Immanuel" [which means "God with us."] (Isaiah 7:14).
  Fulfillment: "When His mother Mary had been betrothed to Joseph, before they came together she was found to be with child from the Holy Spirit" (Matthew 1:18).

The Messiah would enter Jerusalem on a donkey colt.
  Prophecy: "Rejoice greatly, O daughter of Zion! Shout aloud, O daughter of Jerusalem! Behold, your king is coming to you; righteous and having salvation is He, humble and mounted on a donkey, on a colt, the foal of a donkey" (Zechariah 9:9).
  Fulfillment: "And they brought it to Jesus, and throwing their cloaks on the colt, they set Jesus on it. And as He rode along, they spread their cloaks on the road. As He was drawing near—already on the way down the Mount of Olives—the whole multitude of His disciples began to rejoice and praise God with a loud voice for all the mighty works that they had seen, saying, 'Blessed is the King who comes in the name of the Lord! Peace in heaven and glory in the highest!'" (Luke 19:35–38).

The Messiah would be betrayed for thirty pieces of silver.
Prophecy: "Then I said to them, 'If it seems good to you, give me my wages; but if not, keep them.' And they weighed out as my wages thirty pieces of silver. Then the LORD said to me, 'Throw it to the potter'—the lordly price at which I was priced by them. So I took the thirty pieces of silver and threw them into the house of the LORD, to the potter" (Zechariah 11:12–13).
Fulfillment: "And they paid him thirty pieces of silver. . . . And throwing down the pieces of silver into the temple, he departed. . . . So they took counsel and bought with them the potter's field" (Matthew 26:15; 27:5, 7).

The Messiah would be patient and silent under suffering.
Prophecy: "He was oppressed, and He was afflicted, yet He opened not His mouth; like a lamb that is led to the slaughter, and like a sheep that before its shearers is silent, so He opened not His mouth" (Isaiah 53:7).
Fulfillment: "But when He was accused by the chief priests and elders, He gave no answer. Then Pilate said to Him, 'Do You not hear how many things they testify against You?' But He gave him no answer, not even to a single charge, so that the governor was greatly amazed" (Matthew 27:12–14).

The Messiah would be numbered with the transgressors.
Prophecy: "He poured out His soul to death and was numbered with the transgressors" (Isaiah 53:12a).
Fulfillment: "And with Him they crucified two robbers, one on His right and one on His left" (Mark 15:27).

The Messiah would make intercession for His murderers.
Prophecy: "He bore the sin of many, and makes intercession for the transgressors" (Isaiah 53:12b).
Fulfillment: "Jesus said, 'Father, forgive them, for they know not what they are doing'" (Luke 23:34).

None of His bones would be broken.
Prophecy: "He keeps all His bones; not one of them is broken" (Psalm 34:20).

Fulfillment: "But when they came to Jesus and saw that He was already dead, they did not break His legs.... For these things took place that the Scripture would be fulfilled: 'Not one of His bones will be broken'" (John 19:33, 36).

The Messiah would be buried with the rich.
Prophecy: "And they made His grave with the wicked and with a rich man in His death" (Isaiah 53:9).
Fulfillment: "There came a rich man... named Joseph.... He went to Pilate and asked for the body of Jesus.... And Joseph took the body and wrapped it in a clean linen shroud and laid it in his own new tomb" (Matthew 27:57–60).

The Messiah would sit at the right hand of God.
Prophecy: "The LORD says to my Lord: 'Sit at My right hand, until I make Your enemies Your footstool'" (Psalm 110:1).
Fulfillment: "He sat down at the right hand of the Majesty on high" (Hebrews 1:3).

The Messiah would be called the Son of Man with all dominion.
Prophecy:

"I saw in the night visions,
    and behold, with the clouds of heaven
there came one like a son of man,
    and He came to the Ancient of Days
and was presented before Him.

And to Him was given dominion
    and glory and a kingdom,
that all peoples, nations, and languages
    should serve Him;
His dominion is an everlasting dominion,
    which shall not pass away,
and His kingdom one that shall not be destroyed." (Daniel 7:13–14).

Fulfillment: "But that you may know that the Son of Man has authority on earth to forgive sins" (Mark 2:10).

These are just twelve examples of the numerous messianic prophecies Jesus fulfilled, but those mentioned above should enable us to recognize that the fulfillment of messianic prophecy by Jesus provides powerful evidence that He really is the promised Messiah of God. Jesus' fulfillment of prophecy also allows us to understand what the historian Luke was explaining when he said that the evangelist Apollos "refuted the Jews in public, showing by the Scriptures [Old Testament] that the Christ was Jesus" (Acts 18:28).

THE STORY OF LOUIS LAPIDES

There is no question that Jesus' fulfillment of Old Testament prophecy has been a major factor in people becoming believers, including people in our time. Louis Lapides is one such example. While in his mid-twenties on the Sunset Strip in West Hollywood, Louis met a small group of Christians who were handing out Bibles to anyone who would take them. Louis told the Christians that as a Jew he had no interest in the Christian Bible. One of them replied that he should only read the Old Testament, and it would lead him to the Messiah, who was Jesus Christ. Louis then accepted the Bible and went on his way.

> Jesus' fulfillment of Old Testament prophecy has been a major factor in people becoming believers, including people in our time.

After returning home, he began to read, starting with Genesis. The more Louis read, the more he realized that the messianic prophecies of the Old Testament provide a detailed picture of one man—Jesus of Nazareth. He came to Isaiah 53 and read:

> Surely He has borne our griefs
>   and carried our sorrows;
> yet we esteemed Him stricken,
>   smitten by God, and afflicted.
> But He was pierced for our transgressions,
>   He was crushed for our iniquities;
> upon Him was the chastisement that brought us peace,
>   and with His wounds we are healed.
> All we like sheep have gone astray;
>   we have turned—every one—to his own way;
> and the LORD has laid on Him
>   the iniquity of us all. (Isaiah 53:4–6)

Louis saw that this was clearly a prophecy of Jesus of Nazareth. In an attempt to deal with this prophecy, he contacted his stepmother and asked her to send him a Jewish Bible so he could read that instead. He then began reading the Jewish Bible and quickly concluded that it read just like the Bible he had been given! With that realization, said Louis, he aggressively continued his search for the truth about Jesus and subsequently converted to Christianity.[48]

Some years later, Louis was asked if there was any possibility that these messianic prophecies could refer to anyone else. In answer, he said that the odds for someone to fulfill all the Old Testament messianic prophecies are astronomical. Nevertheless, he stated, Jesus, and only Jesus, managed to do so.[49] The chances of Jesus having fulfilled the messianic prophecies strictly by chance is essentially zero. The only reasonable conclusion is that the long-awaited and promised Messiah has come into the world, and His name is Jesus of Nazareth. In addition, once the Old Testament prophets were established as true prophets, then their prophecies were established as true as well. Jesus' fulfillment of these true prophecies, in this case the messianic prophecies, demonstrates that He truly is the promised and long-awaited Messiah.

We do well to follow the example of Jesus Himself in using His fulfillment of prophecies to demonstrate that He truly is the promised Messiah. On the road to Emmaus, He said:

> "O foolish ones, and slow of heart to believe all that the prophets have spoken! Was it not necessary that the Christ should suffer these things and enter into His glory?" And beginning with Moses and all the Prophets, He interpreted to them in all the Scriptures the things concerning Himself. (Luke 24:25–27)

If Jesus proclaimed the Gospel message while also providing evidence to His listeners that verified the truth of His message, perhaps we should too.

It should be mentioned that theological liberals and skeptics commonly argue that the many prophecies in the Old Testament were written after the events they described took place. They argue this because they assume genuine prophecy can't happen. For instance, these individuals say that the Book of Daniel (530 BC) must have been written after the time of Alexander the Great (356–323 BC) because Daniel described Alexander in unmistakable detail. The skeptics' denial of prophecy, however, is disproved by the many explicit messianic prophecies fulfilled by Jesus of Nazareth since it is known beyond a doubt that the entire Old Testament was written before the coming

---

48 Louis Lapides tells his story in *Who Is Jesus? Building a Comprehensive Case*, a DVD from Focus on the Family's *The Truth Project*.

49 Lapides, *Who Is Jesus?*

of Christ.[50] As mentioned above, therefore, Jesus' fulfillment of the messianic prophecies validates not only His own authenticity, but that of the Old Testament prophets as well.[51]

POSTSCRIPT

Before leaving the topic of Jesus' fulfillment of the messianic prophecies, we should note that He, too, made remarkable prophecies that were fulfilled. One of Jesus' most dramatic predictions was that Jerusalem would be destroyed and the temple would be so completely demolished that, He said, "There will not be left here one stone upon another that will not be thrown down" (Matthew 24:2). In view of this impending devastation of Jerusalem, Jesus told His followers to take the following action:

> But when you see Jerusalem surrounded by armies, then know that its desolation has come near. Then let those who are in Judea flee to the mountains, and let those who are inside the city depart, and let not those who are out in the country enter it, for these are days of vengeance, to fulfill all that is written. Alas for women who are pregnant and for those who are nursing infants in those days! For there will be great distress upon the earth and wrath against this people. They will fall by the edge of the sword and be led captive among all nations, and Jerusalem will be trampled underfoot by the Gentiles, until the times of the Gentiles are fulfilled. (Luke 21:20–24)

This terrible destruction of Jerusalem took place in AD 70. The Roman army marched against the city, and wanting not only to put down the Jewish rebellion but also to make an example of it, the Romans killed or enslaved every inhabitant of the city. They so totally destroyed the temple that not one stone was left upon another, just as Jesus said would happen.

Several of the Early Church Fathers reported that the Christians, however, had fled the city before its destruction, just as Jesus had instructed them, so they were spared.[52] The Christians fled even though doing so was contrary to conventional wisdom. Citizens of nations being invaded would normally

---

50 The Dead Sea Scrolls (some of which date back to the fourth century BC) predate the coming of Jesus and contain much of the Old Testament, as does the translation of the Old Testament from Hebrew into Greek known as the Septuagint (second and third centuries BC). The New Testament writers commonly quoted from the Septuagint.

51 See 2 Peter 1:19.

52 Both Eusebius (AD 260–340) and Epiphanias (AD 315–405) mention this. For more, see Scott, "Did Jerusalem Christians Flee to Pella?"

retreat to the fortified cities and stay there because they would then have the protection of the city walls and the added protection of the military personnel stationed there.

Fortunately, Jesus' followers heeded His instructions, not the strategy that was normally called for. In contrast to what threatened people almost always did, the Christians did exactly the opposite. They did what Jesus told them to do "when you see Jerusalem surrounded by armies" (v. 20). But isn't it too late to escape when the city is surrounded? How did the Christians flee when the city was already under siege? In his book *The Wars of the Jews*, the historian Josephus answered that question. He wrote: "Cestius [the Roman commander] . . . retreated from the city without any just occasion in the world."[53]

This unexpected retreat gave the Christians their opportunity to leave the city, which they did. Josephus recorded, however, that the Roman army soon returned and then destroyed the city.[54] We can see, therefore, that the secular historian Josephus not only recorded that Jesus' prophecy was fulfilled exactly as He had predicted, but Josephus additionally provided us with details the Bible didn't give us; he explained how the Christians were able to escape. We should be sure to recognize that both Jesus' prophecy, and Luke's reporting of it, took place before Jerusalem was destroyed.

We can see, therefore, that Jesus' prophecy was accurate and that His followers were saved by His protecting hand. That is, we can see that it was only by the God-man's supernatural power, the power of Him who rules over the nations, that His people were spared.

---

53   Josephus, *Works of Josephus*, 496.
54   Josephus, *Works of Josephus*, 497–98.

QUESTIONS FOR REVIEW AND DISCUSSION

1. How might someone try to explain the similarities between the messianic prophecies and Jesus' life and death without concluding that Jesus is the promised Messiah?

2. We have seen that the promise of the coming Messiah is the unifying theme of the entire Old Testament. What do you think is the unifying theme of the New Testament?

CHAPTER 8

THE RESURRECTION AND ALTERNATE THEORIES

We now come to the primary proof that Jesus of Nazareth is the promised Messiah: His resurrection from the dead. Early in His earthly ministry, Jesus was asked to provide evidence that He had the authority to drive the money-changers out of the temple. The conversation went like this:

> So the Jews said to Him, "What sign do You show us for doing these things?" Jesus answered them, "Destroy this temple, and in three days I will raise it up." The Jews then said, "It has taken forty-six years to build this temple, and will You raise it up in three days?" But He was speaking about the temple of His body. When therefore He was raised from the dead, His disciples remembered that He had said this, and they believed the Scripture and the word that Jesus had spoken. (John 2:18–22)

And on Mars Hill, Paul relied on the resurrection as the primary evidence for showing that Jesus was the Messiah. Paul said,

> The times of ignorance God overlooked, but now He commands all people everywhere to repent, because He has fixed a day on which He will judge the world in righteousness by a man whom He has appointed; and of this He has given assurance to all by raising Him from the dead. (Acts 17:30–31)

At the same time, the resurrection is one the chief doctrines of the Christian faith. Paul also said,

> That is why his [Abraham's] faith was "counted to him as righteousness." But the words "it was counted to him" were not written for his sake alone, but for ours also. It will be counted to us who believe in Him who raised from the dead Jesus our Lord, who

was delivered up for our trespasses and raised for our justification. (Romans 4:22–25)

Here, Paul explained that the resurrection was God's proclamation that because of Jesus' perfect life and substitutionary death for us, God has declared that the sins of all people are forgiven. His word is all-powerful. We are all forgiven. We are now invited to receive this forgiveness by faith.

We also note that the three ecumenical creeds—the Apostles', Nicene, and Athanasian Creeds—all emphasize the resurrection of the Christ as one of the central tenets of the Christian faith. In the resurrection, Christian doctrine and Christian apologetics come together. The resurrection is central to both.

PAUL'S ARGUMENT FOR THE RESURRECTION

The Bible and other sources give us powerful and convincing evidence for recognizing that the resurrection is true, that it really happened in genuine history.[55] We begin with the argument of the apostle Paul, who said,

> For I delivered to you as of first importance what I also received: that Christ died for our sins in accordance with the Scriptures, that He was buried, that He was raised on the third day in accordance with the Scriptures, and that He appeared to Cephas, then to the twelve. Then He appeared to more than five hundred brothers at one time, most of whom are still alive, though some have fallen asleep. Then He appeared to James, then to all the apostles. Last of all, as to one untimely born, He appeared also to me. For I am the least of the apostles, unworthy to be called an apostle, because I persecuted the church of God. But by the grace of God I am what I am, and His grace toward me was not in vain. On the contrary, I worked harder than any of them, though it was not I, but the grace of God that is with me. Whether then it was I or they, so we preach and so you believed.
>
> Now if Christ is proclaimed as raised from the dead, how can some of you say that there is no resurrection of the dead? But if there is no resurrection of the dead, then not even Christ has been raised. And if Christ has not been raised, then our preaching is in

---

55 "Other sources" include Early Church leaders such as Clement of Rome, Polycarp, Ignatius, and Tertullian, as well as secular or non-Christian sources such as Josephus, Tacitus, and the Jewish Talmud.

vain and your faith is in vain. We are even found to be misrepresenting God, because we testified about God that He raised Christ, whom He did not raise if it is true that the dead are not raised. For if the dead are not raised, not even Christ has been raised. And if Christ has not been raised, your faith is futile and you are still in your sins. Then those also who have fallen asleep in Christ have perished. If in Christ we have hope in this life only, we are of all people most to be pitied.

But in fact Christ has been raised from the dead, the firstfruits of those who have fallen asleep. For as by a man came death, by a man has come also the resurrection of the dead. For as in Adam all die, so also in Christ shall all be made alive. But each in his own order: Christ the firstfruits, then at His coming those who belong to Christ. Then comes the end, when He delivers the kingdom to God the Father after destroying every rule and every authority and power. (1 Corinthians 15:3–24)

This portion of Paul's epistle is far more than just a statement that Christ has risen from the dead; it is actually a sophisticated line of argument (as we will explore in the following paragraphs) with convincing evidence that the resurrection is true. We also observe that Paul was making this argument to refute the claim that there is no resurrection from the dead. The Jewish Sadducees, as we know, denied Jesus' resurrection. It may be that their influence had spread to the Church in Corinth. We also recognize that many in our day deny the resurrection as well—or, at least, they are unsure whether the resurrection actually happened. We can easily see here, therefore, that two of the most important uses of apologetics are refuting false doctrine—especially the assertion that Jesus was not raised from the dead—and answering important questions. Such questions include the problem of evil, disagreements about the date of composition for New Testament books, and the status of Gnostic writings (second century and later accounts) such as the Gospel of Thomas and the Gospel of Mary.

> Two of the most important uses of apologetics are refuting false doctrine . . . and answering important questions.

Paul began his argument by reminding his readers that Jesus fulfilled the messianic prophecies, specifically the prophecy that the Messiah would die and be raised from the dead. Paul said, "Christ died for our sins in accordance with the Scriptures, that He was buried, that He was raised on the third day in accordance with the Scriptures" (vv. 3–4).

Paul then presented an impressive list of people to whom Jesus had appeared after His resurrection. These individuals include Peter, then all of the twelve disciples, more than five hundred of their company at the same time, then His brother James, then all the apostles, and finally Paul himself. Paul personally knew many of these individuals, and he knew them well. As a consequence, when Paul said that these individuals had seen the risen Christ, there was very good reason to believe him. In addition, Paul was telling his readers that if they weren't sure that Jesus had risen, they could ask any of these other people who had seen him. Imagine a court of law where one side brought in hundreds of people to give eyewitness testimony to establish what that side said had taken place. The other side would have to acknowledge that position as established fact and then try to plead its case in a way that would not challenge what was known to have happened.

Paul first established the truth that Jesus had risen from the dead. He then proceeded to the question at hand. He rhetorically asked: "Now if Christ is proclaimed as raised from the dead, how can some of you say that there is no resurrection of the dead?" (v. 12). He then immediately proceeded from the conclusion he had just established to the following deductive argument:

First premise: If Christ has been raised from the dead, then the resurrection from the dead is true.

Second premise: Christ has been raised from the dead.

Conclusion: Therefore, the resurrection from the dead is true.

This argument is valid; the first premise is self-evident while the second premise has been established by evidence.[56] Paul then proceeded to another deductive argument. It has this form:

First premise: But if there is no resurrection, then Christ has not been raised.

Second premise: Some of you say there is no resurrection.

Conclusion: Then some of you must also say that Christ has not risen.

The first premise is obvious. The second premise consists of the false doctrine Paul was refuting, and the conclusion necessarily follows from the premises because, once again, the argument is valid. To say there is no resurrection is also to say that Jesus was not raised.

Paul used the conclusion just established to show that if Jesus has not

---

56   This is the common hypothetical ("If, then") type of syllogism (deductive argument). A deductive argument contains a conclusion based on premises. If the premises of such an argument are true, and if the argument takes the proper form (i.e., is valid), then the conclusion must be true.

been raised, then Paul and the members of the Corinthian congregation are wasting their time being believers—and worse: if Jesus has not been raised, they are misrepresenting God. We won't describe the remainder of Paul's arguments in such detail, even though we could easily do so, but suffice it to say that Paul's arguments are valid, and the premises either follow from what Paul has already established or are self-evident. We need to recognize, as well, that deductive arguments are like mathematics; such arguments are like two plus two equals four. If the premises are accurate and the reasoning is sound, then you know for certain that the conclusion is true.

After establishing the truth of the resurrection, Paul then immediately proceeded to the glorious Gospel message:

> But in fact Christ has been raised from the dead, the firstfruits of those who have fallen asleep. For as by a man came death, by a man has come also the resurrection of the dead. For as in Adam all die, so also in Christ shall all be made alive. (vv. 20–22)

Paul presented a series of arguments, all being crystal clear and valid, as a demonstration that the resurrection of Christ and of all believers is certain and true. His arguments are sophisticated and based on conclusions supported by the overwhelming evidence of the messianic prophecies, extensive eyewitness testimony, and self-evident truths.[57] Even the skeptics have a difficult time getting around the overall conclusion Paul presented here.[58]

HISTORICAL DOCUMENTS THAT SUPPORT THE RESURRECTION

We possess five separate historical documents that are also biblical and that clearly state that Jesus did, in fact, rise from the dead. (We will evaluate the reliability of these documents in the next chapter.) They are the historical records of Matthew, Mark, Luke, John, and Paul. We keep in mind once again that just because a document is included in the Bible, this does not in any way reduce its value as a historical document.

We also have a number of nonbiblical documents that clearly state Jesus' resurrection from the dead. One such written record comes from Clement of Rome (AD 30–100), who could well be the Clement to whom Paul referred in Philippians 4:3. Clement had been instructed by the apostles themselves, so

---

57 There are hundreds of arguments described in the Scriptures. I have never seen a fallacious argument advanced by Jesus or the authors of any of the books of the Bible. The enemies of the faith, in contrast, consistently used faulty arguments, usually arguments based on false premises.
58 Habermas and Licona, *Case for the Resurrection*, 49–50.

he would have known what they said regarding the resurrection. Clement stated,

> [The apostles] having therefore received their orders, and being fully assured by the resurrection of our Lord Jesus Christ, and established in the word of God, with full assurance of the Holy Ghost, they went forth proclaiming that the Kingdom of God was at hand.[59]

In this way, Clement explained that the apostles knew Jesus had risen. He also said that the reason their lives were completely transformed was because of the resurrection and also because of the power of the Holy Spirit.

Similarly, Polycarp (AD 69–156) stated unequivocally that Jesus had risen from the dead. Like Clement of Rome, Polycarp had been instructed by the apostles themselves. Polycarp actually referred to the resurrection six times in his letter to the Church at Philippi. Like Clement, as an associate and student of the eyewitnesses, Polycarp was in an excellent position to know what had happened. Polycarp said: "For they loved not this present world, but Him who died for us, and for our sakes was raised again by God from the dead."[60]

Ignatius (AD 35–108) was another close associate of the apostles who claimed they had seen and touched Jesus after His resurrection. In his letter to the Church at Smyrna, Ignatius said,

> For I know that after His resurrection He still possessed of the flesh, and I believe that He is so now. When, for instance, He came to those who were with Peter, He said to them, "Lay hold, handle me, and see that I am not an incorporeal spirit." And immediately they touched Him, and believed, being convinced both by His flesh and spirit. For this cause also they despised death, and were found its conquerors. And after His resurrection He did eat and drink with them, so being possessed of flesh, although spiritually He was united to the Father.[61]

Because Clement, Polycarp, and Ignatius wrote shortly after the resurrection of Christ, and because they were personal associates of the eyewitnesses themselves, their testimonies carry enormous historical credibility. They had every reason to know what the apostles believed had happened. In addition, the apostles themselves, as eyewitnesses of everything Jesus had

---

59 Clement, "Epistle to the Corinthians," 42:3, *Ante-Nicene*, vol. 1, 16.
60 Polycarp, "The Epistle of Polycarp to the Philippians," para. 9, *Ante-Nicene*, vol. 1, 33.
61 Ignatius, "Epistle of Ignatius to the Smyrnaeans," chapter 3, *Ante-Nicene*, vol. 1, 87.

said and done, had every reason to know what had taken place. If Jesus had actually risen, these apostles knew it was so.

Even Jesus' enemies attested to the resurrection by saying that Jesus' disciples had stolen the body—thereby admitting that the tomb was empty and Jesus' body was nowhere to be found. This explanation of thievery is totally unreasonable, however, because a Roman military unit had been assigned to guard the tomb. Matthew used the Greek word κουστωδίαν (*koustodian*) to refer to the Roman guard unit. A *koustodian* was a highly trained guard normally consisting of sixteen disciplined soldiers, each assigned to guard six square feet of space.[62] The penalty for sleeping while on guard duty was death. No one fooled with these Roman guards. Would the frightened and disillusioned disciples have attempted to overcome such a Roman guard? No, and if they had, they would not have succeeded.

In addition, Jesus' enemies tacitly agreed that the tomb was empty. If it hadn't been empty, they would have produced the body and put an end to the testimony of the apostles. The famed Jewish rabbi Gamaliel would have encouraged the Jewish leaders who opposed the apostles to simply produce the body if that had been possible (Acts 5:34–39). His silence on the matter strongly suggests that they all knew the tomb was empty. And the attestations of the Roman guards that the body had been stolen, spoken at the direction of the Jewish leaders, as well as the silence of Gamaliel on the empty tomb, are testimonies of hostile witnesses—those who would have much preferred to say something quite different. Such testimony provides powerful evidence that the tomb was indeed empty.

We even have non-Christian historical records that allude to the resurrection of the Christ. One of these references comes from. In his historical accounts, Josephus wrote:

> At this time there was a wise man who was called Jesus. And his conduct was good and was known to be virtuous. And many people from among the Jews and other nations became his disciples. Pilate condemned him to be crucified and to die. And those who had become his disciples did not abandon his discipleship. They reported that he had appeared to them three days after his crucifixion and that he was alive; accordingly he was perhaps the messiah concerning whom the prophets have recounted wonders.[63]

---

62 Thayer, *Greek-English Lexicon*, 358.
63 Josephus, *Works of Josephus*, 379. Note: This text actually says "He was the Christ." Because this language is disputed by those who say this wording must have been added by a Christian writer, the author has, at this one point, used the language of the Arabic version of Josephus instead,

This statement from Josephus establishes the following historical facts about Jesus:
1. A man called "Jesus" lived in Palestine in the early first century.
2. He was known to be a good and virtuous man.
3. Many people, both Jews and Gentiles, became His followers.
4. He was sentenced to death by crucifixion by Pontius Pilate.
5. The movement He began continued after His death.
6. Jesus' own disciples (the eyewitnesses) claimed He had risen from the dead.
7. Many people, both Jews and Gentiles, believed He was the promised Messiah.

Perhaps the most significant fact established by Josephus is that it was Jesus' own disciples who claimed He had risen from the dead. They said that He was, therefore, the Messiah. That is, it was the eyewitnesses of the important events—those who were there, those who were in a position to know what had actually happened because they had firsthand knowledge—who said He had risen and that He was, therefore, God in the flesh, the King of kings and Lord of lords. Is there any reason to doubt the historical accuracy of these eyewitnesses to whom Josephus referred? There really isn't—especially because, as we have already observed, they faced death rather than change their story. People don't die for what they know is a lie.

> People don't die for what they know is a lie.

The Roman historian Tacitus (AD 55–117) also referred to Jesus' resurrection. In addition to being a historian, Cornelius Tacitus was also a Roman senator, a consul, and a governor of Asia. Like Josephus, Tacitus was a prominent Roman leader as well as being a trustworthy historian. He said:

> Nero fastened the guilt [for the fire of Rome in AD 64] and inflicted the most exquisite tortures on a class hated for their abominations, called Christians by the populace. Christus, from whom the name had its origin, suffered the extreme penalty during the reign of Tiberius at the hands of one of our procurators, Pontius Pilatus, and a most mischievous superstition, thus checked for

---

which says, "He was perhaps the Messiah." There is a fair amount of agreement that Josephus said at least this much. See Habermas and Licona, *Case for the Resurrection*, 266–70.

the moment, again broke out not only in Judaea, the first source of the evil, but even in Rome.[64]

The "mischievous superstition" of which Tacitus spoke is obviously the belief in the resurrection of Jesus. This account by Tacitus supports and is totally consistent with the records of Josephus, the leaders of the Early Church, and the New Testament documents. There is no reason to doubt what any of these historical documents say—other than an ironclad preconceived notion that it didn't happen.

THE TRANSFORMED LIVES OF THE DISCIPLES

As mentioned above, the resurrection of Jesus explains why the disciples were totally changed personalities shortly after the crucifixion. They were transformed from frightened cowards—one of them being too terrified to even give an honest answer to a servant girl while most of the others were in hiding—to courageous witnesses of the resurrection, which they said had brought about their unshakable conviction that Jesus was the Messiah of God. And this was a conviction so certain that they were willing to face death rather than change their story.

The remarkable change in the disciples did not go unnoticed. Luke recorded that even the enemies of the disciples were impressed by it. Luke wrote, "Now when they saw the boldness of Peter and John, and perceived that they were uneducated, common men, they were astonished. And they recognized that they had been with Jesus" (Acts 4:13).

How can we explain this remarkable change in the behavior of the disciples? Luke described the reason for the change:

> [Jesus] presented Himself alive to them after His suffering by many proofs, appearing to them during forty days and speaking about the kingdom of God.
>
> And while staying with them He ordered them not to depart from Jerusalem, but to wait for the promise of the Father, which, He said, "you heard from Me; for John baptized with water, but you will be baptized with the Holy Spirit. . . . You will receive power when the Holy Spirit has come upon you, and you will be My witnesses in Jerusalem and in all Judea and Samaria, and to the end of the earth." (Acts 1:3–5, 8)

The lives of the disciples were totally transformed because Jesus appeared to

---

64   Tacitus, 380.

them after His resurrection over a period of forty days and provided "many proofs" that He was alive (v. 3). He then filled them with the Holy Spirit so they could accurately and courageously proclaim the truth that Jesus had risen from the dead and that He was, therefore, the promised Messiah of God (vv. 4–5).

The dramatic change in James is especially noteworthy. John informed us that James was not a believer during Jesus' earthly ministry. John writes: "For not even His brothers believed in Him" (John 7:5). But we learn that after the ascension of Christ, James was a leader of the Early Church in Jerusalem (Acts 13:12–21). What changed? Paul answered that question when he explained: "Then He [Jesus] appeared to more than five hundred brothers at one time, most of whom are still alive, though some have fallen asleep. Then He appeared to James, then to all the apostles" (1 Corinthians 15:6–7). James's life was totally transformed because he had personally seen the risen Christ! And James was so firm in his belief in Jesus' divinity that he suffered martyrdom for his faith as attested to by Josephus and others.[65]

Being eyewitnesses of the resurrection and being equipped by the Spirit of God remade these disciples into bold, articulate, selfless, and highly sophisticated spokesmen for the truth of the Gospel message. Being eyewitnesses and being equipped by the Holy Spirit additionally enabled these apostles to write the books of our New Testament.

ALTERNATE THEORIES FOR THE EMPTY TOMB

As mentioned above, there is one important reality everyone in Jesus' time agreed on—the tomb was empty. If it hadn't been empty, there would be no Christianity. And because it was empty, skeptics have had to find alternative theories to explain the reason it was empty. In addition to the fanciful notion that the disciples stole the body, which we have already dismissed, there have been other hypotheses presented to explain the empty tomb. Following are several of them:

THE SWOON THEORY

Simply put, this theory states that Jesus didn't die. The idea is that Jesus fainted on the cross but didn't die, and the Roman soldiers took Him down thinking He was dead. Jesus then revived in the tomb, rolled away the stone by Himself (a stone that would have weighed several tons), came out of the grave victorious, overcame sixteen Roman guards, and convinced His

---

[65] Josephus and several Early Christian writers state that James was martyred for his faith. See "The Death of James the Just, Brother of Jesus Christ," *Christian History for Everyman*, accessed June 30, 2017, www.christian-history.org/death-of-james.html.

followers that He had died and then rose from the dead and that He was, accordingly, the Lord of Life.

Like all of these alternate theories, the Swoon Theory is difficult to take seriously. It assumes that the Roman soldiers, who were trained to kill people—and were very good at it—couldn't tell the difference between a dead man and a live one. This theory also requires that this badly beaten man, after hanging on a cross for hours and suffering considerable blood loss, would revive in the tomb all on His own, roll away the stone, single-handedly overpower every Roman guard, perhaps tie them up with the linen cloths He had been buried in so they couldn't chase Him, and then convince His disciples that He had in fact died and then subsequently rose victoriously from the dead. This theory is easily dismissed as pure fantasy.

THE WRONG TOMB THEORY

Another theory states that the women who witnessed the empty tomb simply went to the wrong tomb. If that is the case, then Peter and John went to the wrong tomb, the other disciples went to the wrong tomb, and so did all of Jesus' enemies. If this theory is true, *everyone* went to the wrong tomb. And if all these individuals went to the wrong tomb, this means that the men who buried Jesus had forgotten where they buried Him only three days before. What are the chances these men would have forgotten where they buried someone after only three days?

How, then, do we explain why Jesus' disciples would insist that He had appeared to them after the resurrection? How do we explain Thomas having touched Him, Jesus having eaten in the disciples' presence, and Jesus' ascent into heaven? And why didn't anyone ever discover the right tomb? Once again, telling the difference between real history and pure fantasy is not very difficult.

THE HALLUCINATION THEORY

Given that the disciples were convinced of Jesus' resurrection from the dead, some skeptics have suggested the disciples had hallucinations to that effect—that they didn't actually see the risen Christ. Once again, problems with this theory abound. It is true that people can have hallucinations, but what are the chances that all twelve disciples would have them? And what are chances they would all have the same hallucination and be willing to face severe persecution and even death to defend their hallucination? The answer to those questions is, zero: no chance. In addition, the hallucination theory doesn't begin to explain the empty tomb. Or perhaps the guards also had the hallucination that the tomb was empty. As did the Jewish leaders.

As did the women. As did five hundred other eyewitnesses. Everybody was hallucinating—everybody was crazy!

When we consider the way in which Peter spoke at Pentecost, the content of the Gospels of Matthew and John, and the writings of Paul and of the rest of the New Testament, we are observing the testimony of people who were totally rational and coherent. These were clearly individuals who could tell the difference between fantasy and reality. You may choose to disbelieve what they said, but they were not delusional. The hallucination theory sounds far more like Hollywood than genuine history.

> The hallucination theory sounds far more like Hollywood than genuine history.

After considering these alternative theories, it is no overstatement to conclude that they are simply unbelievable. That is why they have been given little attention here. Truth be told, there is only one reasonable explanation for the information we have, and that is that the resurrection really happened. Jesus really did rise from the dead. The historical evidence that He has risen is quite overwhelming. We have seen that God wants us to proclaim this evidence, just as the apostles did and just as Jesus did Himself. We remember, however, that people don't refuse to believe for lack of evidence. As Jesus Himself said, "If they do not hear Moses and the Prophets, neither will they be convinced if someone should rise from the dead" (Luke 16:31). Jesus was prophesying what the response of many to His own resurrection would be. Once again, the prediction of Jesus has come true.

The failure of the skeptics to come up with any reasonable explanations for the empty tomb, other than the resurrection, and for the fulfillment of this predicted resurrection by Jesus further establishes Him as *the Prophet* of God, the Messiah and King and kings (see Deuteronomy 18:15–18). As Christians, it is our joy to proclaim this truth to the world! And this means we should define our existence and focus our lives on these words Jesus spoke to Mary and Martha, and to us: "I am the resurrection and the life. Whoever believes in Me, though he die, yet shall he live, and everyone who lives and believes in Me shall never die. Do you believe this?" (John 11:25–26).

We say, "Yes, Lord! We believe. Help us in our unbelief."

QUESTIONS FOR REVIEW AND DISCUSSION

1. The story is told of a man who wanted to start a new religion. An acquaintance of his told him, "Jesus of Nazareth died and rose again to found His religion; you could do at least as much." Does this story illustrate an important difference between Christianity and the other religions of the world? Explain. See also Isaiah 41.

2. How does knowing for certain that Jesus rose from the dead influence the way you see death?

CHAPTER 9

EYEWITNESS TESTIMONY AND THE VALIDITY OF THE GOSPELS

The skeptics of Christianity are in a desperate position. They realize they must find an explanation other than the truthfulness of the resurrection for the numerous eyewitness accounts of those who say Jesus really did rise from the dead. They are also at a loss to explain the empty tomb. For these reasons, it's not surprising that the skeptics have for some years now been trying to argue their case from another front. In the United States, beginning in the 1940s and 1950s, the strategy of skeptics and theological liberals has been to assert that the testimony we have about the resurrection is not eyewitness in nature after all, but instead consists of second-century compilations of oral reports that were passed down throughout several generations and were written in order to justify the faith of believers.[66] These second-century accounts, they say, were accepted as being the New Testament because they supported what the Church had come to believe and wanted to teach. Other written accounts were not accepted by the Church, they argue, because they contained theology that differed from what the Church believed. The argument is that the Church created the New Testament and not the other way around.

This means, of course, that Christians for centuries have been lied to. As we have seen, however, the writer of Luke's Gospel said that he wrote down what the eyewitnesses reported and did so only after careful research on his part (Luke 1:1–3). John emphatically said in his Gospel that he was an eyewitness of everything he wrote (John 19:35). Peter said he was an eyewitness (2 Peter 1:16–18), as did Paul (1 Corinthians 15:8), and the Book of Acts explained that the replacement for

> The argument is that the Church created the New Testament and not the other way around.

---

66 This heresy was prevalent in Europe much earlier than this.

Judas had to be an eyewitness of everything from the Baptism of Jesus to His ascension (Acts 1:21-22).

The position of the skeptics, however, is that the writers of all these documents have deliberately misled us; they have lied to us about being eyewitnesses to Jesus' life, death, and resurrection. But why would they do this? None of this explains the empty tomb, of course, but the skeptics wish to divert attention away from that factual reality, as discussed in the previous chapter.

The problem with this position of the skeptics is that the evidence overwhelmingly points in the opposite direction—to the validity of the eyewitness testimony. We will also see the irony of the skeptics' argument in that they accuse the Christian Church of accepting the present New Testament because they liked what these writings said. The truth of the matter is that the skeptics reject the writings of the New Testament documents, not because of serious questions about their authenticity, but rather because the skeptics don't like what the documents say. It is the skeptics who say: "Don't confuse me with facts; my mind is made up." Sadly, however, some church bodies and even many Christian colleges and universities have adopted the heretical position outlined above.

PUTTING THE SKEPTICS' ARGUMENT IN CONTEXT

This position of the skeptics—that the New Testament accounts are not eyewitness in nature—must be viewed in the context of all the other evidence that Jesus is the Messiah. We have seen that the verification of His having worked miracles is so strong that even His enemies admitted to them. Both biblical and nonbiblical sources attest to His miracles. We have seen that His astonishing prophecy about the destruction of Jerusalem and the way the Christians escaped this destruction has been documented by the secular historian Josephus, as well as by scholars of the Early Church. We have seen that Jesus' fulfillment of messianic prophecies was done in such extraordinary detail that the correspondence between the prophecies and the life of Jesus could not be accidental.

We should realize, then, for the above reasons, that the position of the skeptics in denying the apostolic authorship of the New Testament surely appears to be a Hail Mary, resembling the desperate attempt of the New Testament Jewish leaders to find an alternative explanation for Jesus' healing of the man born blind.

In contrast to what skeptics have said, the Gospel writer John spoke with the kind of specificity and clarity that results from having personally been there. John quotes the words of Jesus: "But when the Helper comes, whom

I will send to you from the Father, the Spirit of truth, who proceeds from the Father, He will bear witness about Me. And you also will bear witness, because you have been with Me from the beginning" (John 15:26–27). That is, Jesus told His disciples that they would be the authoritative spokesmen for everything He had said and done because the Spirit of God would guide them into all truth—and because they were eyewitnesses of everything they would proclaim. Jesus also explained that the testimony of these men would be verbally inspired by God and, consequently, would be recognized as inerrant, as outlined above. This is why their writings were accepted by the Church into the New Testament canon, the list of genuine New Testament books.

But is John really the author of the Gospel that bears his name? Bible scholar F. F. Bruce described why all four Gospels were accepted as Scripture by the Early Church:

> One thing must be emphatically stated. The New Testament books did not become authoritative for the Church because they were formally included in a canonical list; on the contrary, the Church included them in her canon because she already regarded them as divinely inspired, recognizing their innate worth and general apostolic authority, direct or indirect.[67]

We remember that for any writing to be apostolic, it must have been written by, or based on, the eyewitnesses themselves. In support of this important criterion, Tertullian (AD 160–220), the preeminent scholar of the New Testament Church, said:

> The same authority of the apostolic churches will afford evidence to the other Gospels also, which we possess equally through their means, and according to their usage—I mean the Gospels of John and Matthew—whilst that which Mark published may be affirmed to be Peter's whose interpreter Mark was. For even Luke's form of the Gospel men usually ascribe to Paul. And it may well seem that the works which disciples publish belong to their masters.[68]

This is an extremely important statement because this brilliant scholar, Tertullian, was explaining why some writings were accepted by the Church while others were not. In dealing with this issue, he explicitly stated that only those accounts written by, or based on the testimony of, the eyewitness-

---

67 Bruce, *The New Testament Documents*, 27.
68 Tertullian, "Against Marcion," book 4, para. 5, *Ante-Nicene*, vol. 1, 350.

Only those accounts written by, or based on the testimony of, the eyewitnesses were accepted by the Early Church.

es were accepted by the Early Church. He identified the Gospels of Matthew and John as having been accepted because they were written directly by eyewitnesses, and the Gospels of Mark and Luke as having been accepted because they were directly based on the accounts of eyewitnesses. In this context, Tertullian also identified other writings as unacceptable because their authorship was unknown or they were written by those who did not have direct eyewitness testimony. We can see, therefore, that the New Testament Church used the same criterion as was stated and used by Peter in Acts 1:21–22 in determining which writings would be accepted as authoritative and reliable and which were not.[69]

This truth cannot be overemphasized: The reason the four Gospels with which we are familiar—Matthew, Mark, Luke, and John—were accepted by the New Testament Church is because the members of the Early Church knew they had been written by the eyewitnesses themselves or were directly based on the accounts of the eyewitnesses.[70] The Church also knew that these men wrote under the guiding hand of the Holy Spirit, as the Holy Spirit had fallen on several of them at Pentecost, and Jesus had said that He would equip them for their work by sending the Holy Spirit to them.[71] We see once again that secondhand information or word-of-mouth accounts were not accepted. In our time, we, too, have the assurance that our New Testament is the account of the eyewitnesses, of those who were there and saw and heard everything with their own eyes and ears. These eyewitnesses have passed their accounts down to us, and they were willing to die for these accounts rather than change their story.

We should also recognize that as time went on, the Church added two additional criteria for canonicity: (1) that the document be consistent with the writings that were already known to be Scripture, and (2) that the document be widely accepted by the various congregations of the New Testament Church. These latter two standards, however, were of far less importance than the primary one, that of eyewitness testimony. However, these

---

69   Paul said: "Am I not an apostle? Have I not seen Jesus our Lord?" (1 Corinthians 9:1) and "Then He appeared to James, then to all the apostles. Last of all, as to one untimely born, He appeared also to me. For I am the least of the apostles, unworthy to be called an apostle, because I persecuted the church of God" (1 Corinthians 15:7–9).

70   See also Luke 1:1–4.

71   Paul explained, "For I would have you know, brothers, that the gospel that was preached by me is not man's gospel. For I didn't receive it from any man, nor was I taught it, but I received it through a revelation of Jesus Christ" (Galatians 1:11–12). See also Acts 1:4–5.

additional criteria are still important for us today because even though the authorship of one book, Hebrews, is still unknown, the first-century Church accepted Hebrews as being apostolic, meaning the authorship would have been known to the first-century Church.[72]

There is even a substantial amount of very early nonbiblical evidence demonstrating that the New Testament is based on eyewitness accounts. Church leader Papias (AD 60–135), a disciple of the apostle John, said:

> Mark, having become the interpreter of Peter, wrote down accurately whatsoever he remembered. It was not, however, in exact order that he related the sayings or deeds of Christ. For he neither heard the Lord nor accompanied Him. But afterwards, as I said, he accompanied Peter, who accommodated his instructions to the necessities [of his hearers], but with no intention of giving a regular narrative of the Lord's sayings. Wherefore, Mark made no mistake in thus writing some things as he remembered them. For one thing he took special care, not to omit anything he had heard and not to put anything fictitious into the statements.[73]

As a contemporary and disciple of John the apostle, Papias would have known why certain writings were accepted by the Early Church and others were not. Similarly, Justin Martyr (AD 100–165) said:

> For the Apostles, in the memoirs composed by them, which are called Gospels, have thus delivered unto us what was enjoined upon them; that Jesus took bread, and when He had given thanks, said, "This do in remembrance of Me."[74]

In this way, Papias and Justin Martyr clarified that the apostles (eyewitnesses who were guided by the Holy Spirit) wrote the Gospels, and for that reason, Justin and his associates regarded these Gospels as authoritative. Justine Martyr lived and wrote before most of the Gnostic gospels were written,[75] and he made it crystal clear that the real Gospels had been written

---

72 Some of the New Testament documents did not include written identification of the author, especially the nonletter books. The epistles are exceptions in that they included the author's name by their very nature. Normally, a cover letter of sorts identified the author, but when the manuscripts were copied, the cover letters often were not, for the New Testament Church knew who wrote the documents, so a cover letter wasn't important to them. We rely on the testimony of Early Church leaders to identify the authorship of several New Testament books.
73 Papias, "Fragments of Papias," *Ante-Nicene*, vol. 1, 154–55.
74 Justin Martyr, "The First Apology of Justin," *Ante-Nicene*, vol. 1, 185.
75 The Gnostic gospels were written in the second, third, and fourth centuries and were not written by the apostles, the eyewitnesses. For that reason, they were never accepted as authoritative by the

by the eyewitnesses themselves. Justin's remarks and comments of other Early Church leaders demonstrate that this theory that the Gospels were not written until the second century is simply contrary to the historical facts.

And there is more. Irenaeus, who was bishop of Lyons in AD 180 and a student of Polycarp, who in turn was a student of the apostle John, said:

> Matthew published his Gospel among the Hebrews in their own tongue, when Peter and Paul were preaching in Rome and founding the church there. After their departure, Mark, the disciple and interpreter of Peter, himself, handed down to us in writing the substance of Peter's preaching. Luke, the follower of Paul, set down in a book the gospel preached by his teacher. Then John, the disciple of the Lord, who also leaned on his breast himself produced his Gospel, while he was living at Ephesus in Asia.[76]

Such statements, along with similar remarks by other leaders in the New Testament Church, give powerful testimony to the eyewitness nature of our biblical documents. These testimonies make it crystal clear that the New Testament Church would accept a book as being authoritative only if it contained the testimony of eyewitnesses.

THE HISTORICAL, GEOGRAPHICAL, AND CULTURAL CONSIDERATION

There is other persuasive evidence that the New Testament is the testimony of the eyewitnesses. That is, we know the books to be historically, geographically, and culturally accurate. The following statement exemplifies the archaeological confirmation of the accuracy in Luke's historical accounts:

> There are literally hundreds of archaeological finds that support specific persons, events and facts presented in Luke-Acts, including many that were once thought to be incorrect. Especially noteworthy is Luke's correct usage of official titles. He calls the rulers of Thessalonica "politarchs," Gallio the "Proconsul of Achaea," the one in Ephesus a "temple warden," the governor of Cyprus a "proconsul," and the chief official in Malta "the first man of the island," a title confirmed in Greek and Latin inscriptions.
>
> Likewise, Luke is known to be correct in chronological references. His reference to "Lysansias the tetrarch of Abiline" at the time John the Baptist began his ministry (AD 27), once thought to be

---

Early Church. They are called "Gnostic gospels" because they promote the Gnostic heresy, which denied the incarnation of Jesus Christ.

76 Irenaeus, "Against Heresies II," *Ante-Nicene*, vol. 1, 258–59.

incorrect, is now known by Greek inscriptions to be correct. Lysansias was tetrarch between AD 14 and 29. Other chronological references are known to be correct including those to Caesar, Herod, and even Gallio (Acts 18:12–17).[77]

This statement provides a small sample of the vast amount of specific details in the New Testament that have been confirmed through modern archaeological research. Gallio, for example, is known to have been proconsul of Achaea from AD 51–52. That is when Paul would have appeared before him, allowing us to date this section of Acts with certainty. Notice especially that Luke called the leader on the Island of Malta the "first man of the island." How could he have known that title if he had not been there? The only reasonable way to account for such accuracy is to recognize that the books contain reliable, firsthand information. Because these documents contain real history—accurate history—they need to be taken seriously.

World-renowned scholar E. M. Blaiklock agrees. After describing the many historical, cultural, political, and geographical details in Acts that have been confirmed by modern research, Blaiklock says that the large number of specific details in the Book of Acts "could have been written only by a first-century historian who spoke naturally in the geographical terminology of contemporary inscriptions."[78] Blaiklock concludes that the view of the skeptics that the Book of Acts was written in the second century has been completely disproved by modern archaeological research.[79]

New Testament scholar F. F. Bruce also commented on the significance of the historical accuracy of Luke-Acts:

> Now, all these evidences of accuracy are not accidental. A man whose accuracy can be demonstrated in matters where we are able to test it is likely to be accurate even where the means for testing him are not available. Accuracy is a habit of mind, and we know from happy (or unhappy) experience that some people are habitually accurate just as others can be depended upon to be inaccurate. Luke's record entitles him to be regarded as a writer of habitual accuracy.[80]

Once again, the only reason for doubting the accuracy of the New Testament's description of Jesus is the ironclad preconceived opinion that it

---

77 Geisler, *Christian Apologetics*, 325.
78 Blaiklock, *Archeology*, 100.
79 Blaiklock, *Archeology*, 100.
80 Bruce, *The New Testament Documents*, 13–14.

The only reason for doubting the accuracy of the New Testament's description of Jesus is the ironclad preconceived opinion that it didn't happen.

didn't happen. In the face of all this evidence to the contrary, have the skeptics been able to maintain their position of second-century authorship of the New Testament? They have not. They have certainly tried to, but have found it impossible to do so.

A SIGNIFICANT SHIFT

Over the years, there has been a profound shift in the position of the skeptics, or at least in the known position of skeptics, generally. In contrast to one or two generations ago, the compelling evidence for the authenticity of many of the New Testament documents has led the vast majority of New Testament scholars, including liberals, skeptics, and atheists, as well as traditionalists, to agree that it indeed was the eyewitnesses themselves who claimed that Jesus had risen from the dead. And it is now recognized that these eyewitnesses made this claim because they were convinced that it really happened. New Testament scholars Gary Habermas and Michael Licona summarized this agreement as follows:

> There is a virtual consensus among scholars who study Jesus' resurrection that, subsequent to Jesus' death by crucifixion, his disciples really believed that he appeared to them risen from the dead. This conclusion has been reached by data that suggest that (1) the disciples themselves claimed that the risen Jesus had appeared to them, and (2) subsequent to Jesus' death by crucifixion, his disciples were radically transformed from fearful, cowering individuals who denied and abandoned him at his arrest and execution into bold proclaimers of the Gospel of the risen Lord. They remained steadfast in the face of imprisonment, torture, and martyrdom. It is very clear that they sincerely believed that Jesus rose from the dead.[81]

How do Habermas and Licona know this to be true? Gary Habermas keeps a list of recognized New Testament scholars of all stripes and what they believe on various theological questions. He can produce the list and easily demonstrate what each of these scholars holds on various issues—including their position on whether it was the apostles themselves who claimed that Jesus had risen from the dead. Because of the consensus Habermas and

---

[81] Taken from *The Case for the Resurrection of Jesus*, 49–50. Copyright © 2004 by Gary R. Habermas and Michael R. Licona. Published by Kregel Publications, Grand Rapids, MI. Used by permission of the publisher. All rights reserved.

Licona describe, the previous liberal and skeptical view—that the Church's belief in the resurrection didn't appear until the second century—is now completely discredited. The evidence is too overwhelming that it was Jesus' own associates, the eyewitnesses themselves, who said He had risen.

As mentioned above, this is a significant change from the views of the skeptics and liberals of one or two generations ago, who commonly claimed (or at least appeared to claim) that the resurrection was a second-century invention. One has to wonder, though, if the religion professors at the various private colleges and universities of our land have gotten the message.

(It should be mentioned that we have not considered here the matter of the accuracy of the New Testament text. The reason for this omission is that critical analysis of the New Testament text has pretty much established its accuracy beyond a reasonable doubt. The issue is no longer a matter of significant debate. An excellent summary of what scholars agree on regarding the integrity of this text, and other areas, is contained in a lecture by New Testament scholar Gary Habermas called "The Resurrection Argument That Changed a Generation of Scholars," which can be viewed in its entirety online. See also Lee Strobel's book *The Case for Christ*. Both resources are included in the bibliography.)

So, the questions are these: Should we believe the people who were there and who were convinced they had personally seen and heard the risen Christ? Should we believe the people who were so convinced that Jesus had risen that they were willing to die for what they believed and said? Should we doubt the resurrection in the face of impressive evidence that it is verifiable history—when there is a consensus among New Testament scholars that the people making these claims were present at the time to verify their accuracy? Or should we believe the skeptics who deny the historicity of the resurrection, those living two thousand years later with no firsthand information to support their views and who doubt, not because of the evidence, but because of their assumption that the resurrection could not have happened? The reasonable path, the all-important path, is to believe the eyewitnesses.

QUESTIONS FOR REVIEW AND DISCUSSION

1. Consider the Jewish leaders who tried to find an explanation for Jesus' healing of the man born blind. How does that view compare with the view of skeptics today who deny the resurrection of Christ?

2. How can we equip our young people with a working knowledge of apologetics before they go off to higher education or the workforce?

CHAPTER 10

HISTORICAL ARTIFACTS

Historical research involves more than the study of written documents. It also includes the study of artifacts—physical objects that tell an important part of a historical story. Court cases typically rely on testimony and exhibits. An exhibit may be a weapon of some kind or some other object; it may also be DNA, a photograph, or some kind of document. Artifacts are like exhibits. Personally, I like to call artifacts "hard facts," the reason being that they are often made of stone or metal and their validity goes way beyond someone's mere opinion. Artifacts tell a story that must be true, though we may not always know exactly what that story is. There are many historical artifacts in the field of Christian apologetics, such as those referencing important people, places, and dates. But two especially important ones provide more substantiation for the accuracy of the New Testament accounts. These artifacts are the ossuary (burial coffin) of James the Just and the Shroud of Turin.

THE JAMES OSSUARY

The first artifact we will consider is an ossuary that was found just outside Jerusalem and announced on October 21, 2002, bearing the name James. An ossuary is a stone box used by Jews in New Testament times for storing the bones of the dead. The body of the deceased was left in a cave for a year, and then the bones were collected and placed in an ossuary. This method of burial was common in cities like Jerusalem because burial space was limited. The name of the dead person was usually engraved on the outside of the ossuary. The James ossuary, the artifact of particular interest here, is made of limestone and is 20 inches long, 12 inches wide on one end and 10 inches wide on the other.[82] This ossuary is similar to that of Caiaphas, the high priest, which can be seen on page 114. The only difference between the two is that the James ossuary was not as ornate.

---

82   Altman, "Report on the James Ossuary." Wikimedia Commons; James Ossuary.

Thousands of these ossuaries have been discovered. The sensational feature of the James ossuary is that on one side it bears an inscription in Aramaic that, translated into English, reads: "James, son of Joseph, brother of Jesus." This means that the writing on the stone box identifies the ossuary as that of James the Just, son of Joseph and brother of Jesus, the founder of Christianity.

James was so prominent that the historian Josephus wrote about him. Josephus said that James was martyred in Jerusalem in AD 62 and that James was the brother of Jesus "who was called Christ."[83] In addition, James was frequently mentioned in the New Testament, including the following reference by Paul in Galatians 1: "Then after three years I went up to Jerusalem to visit Cephas and remained with him fifteen days. But I saw none of the other apostles except James the Lord's brother" (vv. 18–19).

The evidence for the genuineness of this ossuary is incredibly strong. It is known that the ossuary dates back to first-century Palestine and to a time shortly before the destruction of Jerusalem in AD 70. In addition, the ossuary's patina, a superficial discoloration resulting from age that covers the exterior, is exactly the same in the lettering as on the sides of the container. This demonstrates that the lettering and the box are of the same age.[84]

Of particular significance is the fact that James is identified as Jesus' brother. It is extremely unusual to mention a brother of the deceased on an ossuary, and it would have been done only if that brother was a very important person. In this case, Jesus was important—in fact, He was the most important person who ever lived. There have been thousands of ossuaries discovered, and there are only one or possibly two besides the James ossuary that identify the brother of the deceased.

Persons who were very important or wealthy were most likely to have their bones buried in ossuaries. From both the New Testament and Josephus, as mentioned above, we know that James, the brother of Jesus, was a prominent leader in the Early Christian Church in Jerusalem. In this one artifact, therefore, we have powerful testimony to the reality and prominence of both James, the brother of Jesus, and of Jesus Himself.

Below is a photograph of the ossuary of Caiaphas, the high priest at the time of Jesus and before whom Jesus appeared for His trial.[85] Notice the ornate designs on the ossuary that were typical of someone having the prominence

---

83   Josephus, *Works of Josephus*, 423.
84   Joseph M. Holden, "The James Ossuary: The Earliest Witness to Jesus and His Family?" 2012, http://normangeisler.com/the-james-ossuary-the-earliest-witness-to-jesus-and-his-family/.
85   Some individuals believe this to be the ossuary of Joseph the son of Caiaphas.

of a high priest. The rounded top also indicates someone of high standing. Real history comes to life and is verified by such artifacts. The James ossuary is no exception.

OSSUARY OF CAIAPHAS.
The inscription on the ossuary literally reads, "Joseph, son of Caiaphas." Josephus identifies the high priest at the time of Jesus as not only Caiaphas but "Joseph Caiaphas." Josephus tells us additionally that Caiaphas was the Jewish high priest from AD 18–36 (*Antiquities* 18:35). Another ossuary found in the same burial chamber is labeled simply "Caiaphas." Which ossuary contained the bones of Caiaphas, the high priest, is not certain. www.BibleLandsPictures.com / Alamy Stock Photo.

THE SHROUD OF TURIN

A second important artifact is the Shroud of Turin, a rectangular linen cloth measuring 14.5 feet long by 3.7 feet wide that is housed at Turin, Italy, in the chapel of the Cathedral of St. John the Baptist. There are significant indications that this artifact is the actual linen cloth that covered the body of Jesus from the time of His burial until His resurrection.

It is often said that the shroud is the most intensely studied historical artifact of all time, and the evidence of its authenticity is quite overwhelming. It is virtually certain that on this linen cloth is an actual photograph of someone killed by crucifixion, someone who was killed in or around Jerusalem at a time that coincides with the death of Jesus of Nazareth. The most reasonable explanation for this photograph is that it pictures Jesus in the tomb—a photograph that occurred the moment he rose from the dead. The photograph looks to have been produced by an energy source unknown to modern science, energy coming from inside the body itself, an energy that is said to have been released when the body of Jesus was transformed from a dead body into a living body with far different qualities than it had previously. There is no known scientific explanation for how the image on the shroud was formed, or even how it could have been formed.

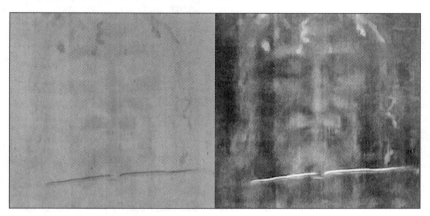

POSITIVE (LEFT) AND NEGATIVE (RIGHT) IMAGES OF THE SHROUD.
Wikimedia Commons, "Shroud positive negative compare"; public domain.

All four Gospels say that a linen cloth was used to wrap the body of Jesus after the crucifixion. Luke, for example, said, "And he [Joseph of Arimathea] took it [the body] down and wrapped it in a linen shroud and laid Him in a tomb cut in stone, where no one had ever yet been laid" (Luke 23:53).

As mentioned, the linen cloth bears the image of a man who was killed by crucifixion. It is significant that the image on the shroud is much clearer in the black-and-white negative than in the photograph's natural sepia color. This negative image of the shroud was first observed in 1898 on the reverse photographic plate of photographer Secondo Pia, the first person to photograph the shroud, and who did so while it was being exhibited in the Turin Cathedral.

There are numerous compelling reasons that point to the genuineness of the shroud as being the actual burial cloth of Jesus. Some of the reasons follow:

1. As Secondo Pia was developing his negatives, he was amazed to see a positive image emerge from his film. (A negative of a negative photograph gives a positive image.) Since it would have been impossible to fake a photographic negative long before the world had any knowledge of photography, there can be no doubt that the shroud contains an actual negative, an actual photograph. As a result, the allegation that the shroud is a painting or fake of some kind is known to be false.

2. The image on the shroud demonstrates that the person was crucified with nails through the wrists, not hands. It was not until 1902 that it became known that the flesh in a person's hands cannot bear the weight necessary for crucifixion; for that reason, nails were driven through the wrists.[86] This means that the shroud is historically accurate regarding the practice of crucifixion even though all the paintings and other works of art of the crucifixion made during the Middle Ages and up until the twentieth century are inaccurate in this regard. (The Greek and Aramaic words for *hands* can also refer to the wrists.)

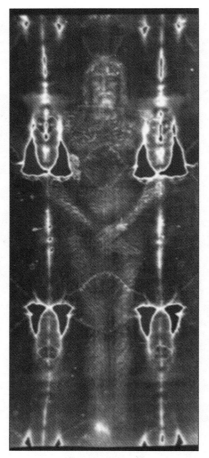

FULL-LENGTH IMAGE ON THE SHROUD.
Wikimedia Commons, "Turin Shroud."

---

86 Wilson and Schwortz, *The Turin Shroud*, 65–67.

3. The energy source for the photograph must have come from within the body itself, one reason being that there are no shadows on the photograph, as would have happened with external lighting. Another indication that the energy source came from the body itself is the fact that the shroud contains the body image from both the front and back sides. External lighting could not make such a photograph.[87]
4. Close inspection of the image on the shroud reveals that it is an x-ray image as well as a photographic image. Skeletal features can be observed. Again, the energy source for the image must have come from within the body, and the source of this energy has no known scientific explanation, which strongly suggests that the energy that produced the image was supernatural.
5. Mideast pollen grains on the shroud, which match certain plant-bearing flowers also pictured on the shroud, are from plants that exist in and around Jerusalem. The identified flowers from these plants are known to bloom in the springtime, the time of Jesus' crucifixion. These clearly identified plants are found as a group only in and around Jerusalem—nowhere else in the world.[88]
6. Written records of the Sudarium of Oviedo (the linen cloth that was used to cover Jesus' head from the time of His death to His burial; so named because it is stored at the Cámara Santa [Holy Chamber] in Oviedo, Spain) go back to the first century and to Jerusalem. The Gospel of John states that two cloths—apparently the shroud and the sudarium—were seen left in the tomb after the resurrection (John 20:6–7). Scientific study of these two linen cloths has revealed that they are stained with same blood type and the stains are the same shapes and are in the same places on both cloths. These two linen cloths covered the same body. There is no image on the sudarium, however, even though it was laying in the tomb along with the shroud. It likely would have been removed when the larger linen cloth was used to cover the body.
7. Some of the pollen grains on the shroud are from a plant that grows in Palestine and is known for its sharp thorns. Those pollen grains are especially numerous around the head of the image on the shroud, apparently left there by the crown of thorns. We

---

[87] For other indications, see Antonacci, *The Resurrection of the Shroud*, 252.
[88] Antonacci, *The Resurrection of the Shroud*, 112.

actually know from the shroud that the thorny vines were formed more into the shape of a cap, not a crown. The thorns and vines covered the top of the head as well as the temples and sides.

8. As mentioned above, the sudarium and the shroud have separate histories, but the blood type and pattern of blood stains and other body fluids all match. For this reason, it is evident that we have two independent but complementary sets of historical records that confirm the authenticity of the shroud.[89]

9. Bruise marks that are a perfect match for those left by a Roman flagrum (a whip used to scourge criminals) are evident on the shroud. These scourge wounds are clearly seen on the back, front, and thighs of the victim of the crucifixion. Bruises on the side of the man's face also match the description of how Jesus was beaten before being crucified.

10. The man pictured on the shroud had been scourged before he was crucified. That was not the common practice in Roman crucifixions. Why would they whip someone they were about to kill? We know, however, that Jesus was scourged by Pilate in the hope that the crowd would have pity on Him so Pilate could let Him go. In addition, the man pictured on the shroud had been crowned with cap of thorns. There is no other record of a crucified man being crowned with thorns. In addition, the crucified man had been stabbed by a lance on the right side. The nature of the lance used to make such a stab wound matches the lances that were common issue for Roman soldiers.

Suffice it to say that the chances of any other man killed by Roman crucifixion matching all these details are extremely remote. The man pictured on the shroud is almost certainly Jesus of Nazareth.[90]

There are numerous other factual indications of the shroud's genuineness in addition to those briefly mentioned above. Many books, periodicals, and websites describe this evidence in considerable detail. Numerous YouTube videos do so as well. The evidence for the authenticity of the shroud is overwhelming. There is no credible evidence of any kind indicating that it is a fraud.

---

89 See also Myra Adams, "The Shroud of Turin, Authenticated Again," *National Review*, April 16, 2016, www.nationalreview.com/article/434153/shroud-turin-jesus-christ-blood-relic-sudarium-oviedo.

90 Even some nonbelievers have come to this conclusion. They may not believe that Jesus is God, but they are convinced that the shroud pictures Him in the tomb.

It should be mentioned, however, that in 1988, a carbon 14 test was done on a small piece of the shroud, and the results indicated that its origin only goes back to the thirteenth or fourteenth century AD. A careful study of that dating process, however, revealed that the piece of cloth used for dating had been taken from a corner of the shroud that had been spliced onto the main cloth to repair damage from a fire. There is at least one peer-reviewed professional journal article by a well-known expert in the relevant fields, chemist Ray Rogers, that demonstrates that the piece of cloth used for the carbon 14 dating was indeed from a fourteenth-century repair. There is really no doubt that this is so. This being the case, there is no known evidence that the shroud is anything other than the burial cloth of Jesus Christ. This also means that the cloth bearing the image is considerably older than the fourteenth century AD, of course. Since the original cloth is now known to be older than the fourteenth century, skeptics seem to have lost interest in conducting another test. In addition, the Catholic Church is reluctant to have another segment of the shroud destroyed as is required by the test. As a consequence, another carbon 14 test is unlikely any time soon.

Since the carbon 14 dating results are now dismissed as meaningless, it is fair to say that the known evidence strongly suggests the shroud is authentic. The evidence is so one-sided that attorney and former agnostic Mark Antonacci said this evidence in great specificity matches the time, place, participants, and other details in the historical accounts of the crucifixion. Antonacci added that this evidence is far superior to that which supports many other important events in history, such as Caesar's crossing of the Rubicon or Martin Luther's nailing of the Ninety-Five Theses to the door of the church at Wittenberg.[91]

Because of the scientific evidence for the authenticity of the shroud, several skeptical scientists and other scholars who were part of the initial scientific study of the shroud have converted to Christianity, as has Antonacci.[92] This should not surprise us because the shroud appears to contain an actual photograph of Jesus of Nazareth the moment He rose from the dead. And, as Paul said, "For I am not ashamed of the gospel, for it is the power of God for salvation to everyone who believes, to the Jew first and also to the Greek" (Romans 1:16).

At the same time, we must recognize that if the shroud is authentic, then it is not possible for science to completely prove it as such—the reason

---

91 Antonacci, *The Resurrection of the Shroud*, 252.
92 Wilson and Schwortz, *The Turin Shroud*, 121.

being that science can only deal with the way nature normally works, and the image on the shroud, if it is genuine, must have been formed in a miraculous manner. Science can only say what the image is not. It cannot say what the image is.

Agreement on details is as far as science can go. To move beyond what science can verify, we must turn to the words of Peter who, after being asked by Jesus the Nazarene, "Who do you say that I am?" replied by confessing: "You are the Christ, the Son of the living God" (Matthew 16:16). We do well to follow his example.

QUESTIONS FOR REVIEW AND DISCUSSION

1. Did you notice the striking similarity between the image on the shroud and the various paintings of Jesus of Nazareth? How might this similarity be explained?

2. The apostle John tells us that right after Jesus raised Lazarus from the dead, "many of the Jews therefore, who had come with Mary and had seen what He did, believed in Him" (John 11:45). Do you think the apparent resurrection pictured on the shroud could have a similar effect in our time? Why or why not?

CHAPTER 11

LOVE WITHOUT LIMITS

While looking at the image on the shroud, a number of people have said they were impressed by the serenity of the man pictured there. How could a person who had just been brutally beaten and then killed by crucifixion look so peaceful? It may be because He knew He had completed His mission, a task described by John the Baptist: "Behold, the Lamb of God, who takes away the sin of the world!" (John 1:29). Jesus knew His mission was complete. That is what He meant when, upon the cross, He said, "It is finished" (19:30).

How could this be? Why would the God of creation be willing to die upon a cross? Why would He consent to be born a baby, and in a stable no less? Why would He consistently go out of His way to help those unfortunate persons who were in need, as symbolized by the actions of the Good Samaritan? Why would He give over some of His precious time and say to the woman at the well at Sychar: "If you knew the gift of God, and who it is that is saying to you, 'Give Me a drink,' you would have asked Him, and He would have given you living water?" (4:10).

> Why would the God of creation be willing to die upon a cross?

Why did He use His valuable time to take the little children into His arms and bless them? Why did He say to the woman caught in adultery, "'Where are they [your accusers]? Has no one condemned you?' She said, 'No one, Lord.' And Jesus said, 'Neither do I condemn you; go, and sin no more'" (8:10). Why did He weep over Jerusalem because of its rejection of Him as well as His knowledge of its coming destruction? Why did He ride into Jerusalem on a donkey when kings rode on majestic horses? Why did He wash His disciples' feet when only servants washed people's feet? Why did He allow Himself to be ridiculed, spit upon, beaten, whipped, and finally crucified? Why did He promise to send the Holy Spirit to us so that we could put our faith in Him, become members of His family as a bride is to her bridegroom, and finally be given eternal life in His presence forever?

All this He did for one reason, and one reason only: His unfathomable love for His people.

Why did He give us an abundance of objective historical evidence so we could see for certain that all this is genuine history, that all this is true?

All this He did for one reason, and one reason only: His unfathomable love for His people. Jesus Christ loves us with a love that we cannot begin to understand. It is a love that is just as great as God is great. It is a love that can be seen or experienced in no other place and in no other person. It is the love of the God-man who was willing to pay any price to bring us out of the depth of our rebellion and sin into eternal fellowship with Him. It is a love that is personally directed from Him to you and to me.

It is a love that captures the theme of the entire biblical message, as stated by His beloved apostle John:

> For God so *loved* the world, that He gave His only Son, that whoever believes in Him should not perish but have eternal life. For God did not send His Son into the world to condemn the world, but in order that the world might be saved through Him. (John 3:16–17, emphasis added)

This is what Jesus' coming was all about. And He leaves us with the question He asked of His other followers: "But who do you say that I am?" (Matthew 16:15). God grant that we answer with Peter, who replied, "You are the Christ, the Son of the living God" (16:16). For by so confessing, we have life in His name.

QUESTIONS FOR REVIEW AND DISCUSSION

1. Do any other religions depict the Almighty as a God of love and grace "who desires all people to be saved and to come to the knowledge of the truth" (1 Timothy 2:4)? Explain.

2. If God is a loving God, why does He allow evil and suffering to exist in this world that He created?

PART 3

ANSWERING OBJECTIONS

CHAPTER 12

THE PROBLEM OF EVIL

We have seen that God is a loving and gracious God who desires nothing but good for the people He created. Why, then, is there evil in the world?

We recognize that the existence of evil has perplexed mankind since the beginning of time. The problem of evil is an objection commonly advanced against Christianity. Countless books and essays have been written about it, many of them composed by some of the best minds the world has known. But in spite of all the attention this problem has received, no one has given the existence of evil a complete and totally satisfactory explanation. In addition, the best minds—believers and skeptics alike—who have grappled with the reality of evil are nowhere near being in agreement on an explanation for it.

At the same time, however, there are significant truths that we can know about the problem. This chapter will focus on what we can know about the issue while at the same time acknowledging there is much that we do not understand. We will confine our focus to seven questions:

1. Does the existence of evil disprove the existence of God?
2. How do atheists explain evil?
3. How do the Scriptures explain the existence of evil?
4. Why does God allow suffering in our lives?
5. Is God unjust in the way He treats us?
6. Does God use our suffering for His purposes and our good?
7. Why did God create a world that He knew would turn to evil?

QUESTION 1: DOES THE EXISTENCE OF EVIL DISPROVE THE EXISTENCE OF GOD?

There are those who say that such is the case, that the reality of evil disproves the existence of God—or at least of a *loving* God. These individuals usually state their argument something like this:

If God is good, He would want to eliminate evil.
If God is almighty, He is able to eliminate evil.
Evil exists.
Therefore, either God is not good or He is not almighty or He does not exist.[93]

The problem of evil is not merely academic; it is very real. Prominent Bible scholar Bart Ehrman says he has concluded that the existence of evil rules out the existence of a loving and all-powerful God. For that reason, says Ehrman, he is no longer a believer.[94] Missionary and apologist Ravi Zacharias said that anyone who minimizes the problem of evil doesn't begin to understand it.[95] The issue clearly has had a major impact on how many people see Christianity and all of life. An acquaintance of mine once put it this way: "If God was real, He would not have allowed my brother to die in Vietnam." Atheist Vexen Crabtree said a good God cannot exist in view of all the pain and suffering in the universe.[96]

> The problem of evil is not merely academic; it is very real.

QUESTION 2: HOW DO ATHEISTS EXPLAIN EVIL?

Before going to the assertion that the problem of evil disproves the existence of God, we should also ask, "How do atheists deal with the problem of evil?" A common answer for atheists is that evil isn't real; evil doesn't exist. In fact, that is what atheists *must* say to be consistent with their worldview. If the world consists of nature plus nothing, which is what atheists believe, then evil cannot be real. Evil becomes nothing more than personal preferences. Prominent atheist-turned-agnostic Richard Dawkins said that in a world of matter and energy, and nothing more, there is no purpose, no good, no evil, nothing but indifference.[97] Dawkins is consistent with his worldview by saying that evil is not real, but as we observed earlier, no one can live this way. In several of his tweets, Richard Dawkins has decried religions that promote violence.[98] But on what grounds can Dawkins object to violence? He is assuming that the kind of violence that occurs with terrorist attacks is evil. Therefore, even Dawkins himself can't live in the world he says he believes, a world without good and evil.

---

93 Craig, "Problem of Evil."
94 Ehrman, "Biblical Views of Suffering."
95 Zacharias, "The Problem of Suffering and the Goodness of God."
96 Crabtree, "The Problem of Evil: Why Would a Good God Create Suffering?"
97 Dawkins, *River Out of Eden*, 131–32.
98 Dawkins, Twitter.

Similarly, before he converted to Christianity, C. S. Lewis said he believed that the existence of evil disproved the existence of God. He believed this until he realized evil couldn't be real without the violation of a moral standard of some kind, and a moral standard couldn't be real without someone to give that moral standard. Consequently, Lewis said he realized his argument against the existence of God actually assumed that God exists.[99]

The problem of evil is actually a greater problem for atheists than for Christians. Atheists are totally caught: either they deny their worldview and recognize evil as real, or they deny common knowledge, their consciences, and their personal experiences to say evil is not real. They have no other option.

Going to the issue itself, is it true that the problem of evil disproves the existence of God? No, it is not. The foremost authority on this matter in our time is Christian philosopher Alvin Plantinga of Notre Dame. (*Time* magazine described Plantinga as the world's most highly regarded Christian philosopher of the orthodox Reformed persuasion.[100]) According to Plantinga, the defect in the argument that evil disproves the existence of God, or at least a loving God, lies in the mistaken assumption that an almighty God can do anything. But, asks Plantinga, can an almighty God create logical contradictions, for example? Can God cease to exist? Can God create free agents who can do what they choose and can only do what God wants at the same time?

As Plantinga sees it, it would appear that God can only do that which is consistent with His nature. It may be, for instance, that God cannot lie and cannot be evil since God is truth and good. It may be that He cannot be evil and good at the same time.

It may be, says Plantinga, that when God created persons—agents who are free—it may be that what happened in the world was then largely up to them. So the question is, Could God create a world with free agents where there would be no possibility of evil? Plantinga says, as far as we know, it may be that such a world is a logical contradiction, which is contrary to God's nature, and is a world that perhaps could not be created.

> Could God create a world with free agents where there would be no possibility of evil?

By analogy, what if you had been living in first-century Rome when slavery was legal? And what if you owned a slave whom you wished to set free, but you had found the slave to be very useful? Could you set the slave free and at the same

---

99 Lewis develops this argument in *Mere Christianity*.
100 "Modernizing the Case for God," *Time*, vol. 115, no. 14 (April 7, 1980), 66.

time be assured that your now former slave would do anything you asked? Obviously you could not. Perhaps the creation of man was like that. Perhaps God's creation of free agents required that they had the capacity to disobey Him. The overall conclusion of Plantinga is not to say what God did do, or could do, but to say that as far as our understanding goes, there is no genuine contradiction in recognizing the existence of a Creator God who is also good despite the existence of evil in the world.[101]

As mentioned above, the problem of evil is a greater problem for atheists than for Christians. It seems odd that those whose materialistic worldview denies the reality of evil also commonly say that evil disproves the existence of God. Obviously, you can't have it both ways.

QUESTION 3: HOW DO THE SCRIPTURES EXPLAIN THE EXISTENCE OF EVIL?

From the Book of Genesis, we can see that God created man in His image, in perfect holiness. God told Adam and Eve they could eat the fruit of any tree—except one. All the trees that God made were good. The fruit of all the trees was good. In fact, God emphasized the unqualified goodness of His creation by stating, at the end of several creation days, that what He had made was good.

The one and only question was whether Adam and Eve would obey God. The question of whether Adam and Eve would obey God's command is similar to one faced by King David. He could have wed any unmarried woman in Israel—anyone he took a fancy to—but no, he had to pick a married woman. The question for David, like the question for Adam and Eve, was primarily one of obedience.

Adam and Eve knew what God had said, but they chose to disobey Him. "The woman said to the serpent, 'We may eat of the fruit of the trees in the garden, but God said, 'You shall not eat of the fruit of the tree that is in the midst of the garden, neither shall you touch it, lest you die'" (Genesis 3:2–3). Unfortunately, Adam and Eve disobeyed God, and mankind has continued to disobey Him ever since.[102]

Paul summarized the tragic consequences of Adam and Eve's disobedience when he said, "Therefore, just as sin came into the world through one man, and death through sin, and so death spread to all men because all

---

101 I had the privilege of studying under Alvin Plantinga some years ago at a six-week summer seminar. The topic was the problem of evil. For that reason, I speak from extensive personal experience in summarizing Plantinga's views.
102 For more on original sin, see the Solid Declaration of the Formula of Concord, Article I, *Concordia: The Lutheran Confessions*.

sinned" (Romans 5:12). Adam and Eve's disobedience had profound consequences on mankind. The nature of being human had changed. In Romans 8:7, Paul said, "For the mind that is set on the flesh is hostile to God, for it does not submit to God's law; indeed, it cannot." Man was now an enemy of God and could only be restored to fellowship with Him by means of a new birth of faith created by the Holy Spirit.[103]

Genesis is emphatic in saying that everything God created was good. Genesis further clarified that evil came into the world because of man's disobedience. Some of the angels had disobeyed God too. The apostle Peter said, "God did not spare angels when they sinned, but cast them into hell" (2 Peter 2:4). So we see that evil in our world is explained by Scripture as the result of the disobedience of Adam and Eve. They had been influenced by Satan.

QUESTION 4: WHY DOES GOD ALLOW SUFFERING IN OUR LIVES?

But what about pain and suffering in the lives of Christians? Why does God allow Christians to suffer? Why doesn't He protect His own people from illnesses and needless pain? Why does He allow bad things to happen to good people? This question is the focus of what may be the oldest book included in the Bible, that being the Book of Job.[104]

Job was a good man who lost almost everything.[105] He lost his possessions. His children and heirs were all killed. His good health was replaced with boils and open sores that tormented him, and even his wife told him he should curse God and die. At this point in Job's story, three of his friends came to be with him during his suffering. These three friends were convinced Job was suffering because he had committed some heinous sin. They repeatedly urged him to come clean and repent of whatever it was he had done. But Job was adamant in insisting he had not committed any awful and particular sin that would warrant the suffering he was experiencing. Job was correct is saying this. God Himself had asked Satan, "Have you considered My servant Job, that there is none like him on the earth, a blameless and upright man, who fears God and turns away from evil?" (Job 1:8).

An important lesson for us in Job, therefore, is that Job was not suffering because of some particular sin on his part. It is the same lesson Jesus taught

---

103 See John 3:1–21.
104 We speak here of the date of writing, not the dates of the events described. Job has the most Hebrew words that appear nowhere else in available recorded literature, including the Bible, suggesting that the time of its writing was earlier than any of the other biblical accounts.
105 Job is pictured as a "good" man in a relative sense; he was "good" compared to other sinful people. He is not pictured as morally upright before God's Holy Law. Romans 3:23 says, "For all have sinned and fall short of the glory of God."

when He said, "Or those eighteen on whom the tower in Siloam fell and killed them: do you think that they were worse offenders than all the others who lived in Jerusalem? No, I tell you; but unless you repent, you will all likewise perish" (Luke 13:4–5). The lesson is the same for us: Our suffering is not necessarily a consequence of some particular sin on our part. Nor should we look at the misfortune of others and assume they are being punished for having done wrong. But all of us need to repent and be forgiven of any and all sins we have committed.

QUESTION 5: IS GOD UNJUST IN THE WAY HE TREATS US?

So, if Job's intense suffering was not the result of some particular sin, then why did God allow him to experience such extraordinary misfortune? Job at one point answered that question by concluding that God must be unjust.[106] Job went so far as to ask God to give him a hearing as in a court of law. Job said that if God would give him such a hearing, he would then prove himself righteous and prove God wrong regarding the way he was being treated.

In doing so, Job became the precursor of all who believe that they understand matters like divine justice, goodness, and mercy better than God does. All those who say that the existence of evil, pain, and suffering disprove the existence of a loving God are actually placing themselves above God in making their judgment. They have a pride problem more than an existence of evil problem. People don't reject God because of evil outside of themselves. They reject God because of their own evil, pride being paramount.

As we know from the Book of Job, God did give him a hearing. At that hearing, God's first question to Job was this: "Where were you when I laid the foundations of the earth?" (Job 38:4). At that point, the debate was over. Job immediately realized that for him to stand in judgment over the all-knowing Creator God was the height of foolishness and arrogance. Several chapters later in Job, God compared Job to the Behemoth and the Leviathan He had made. God did so to demonstrate to Job, and to us, that we are very small in comparison to God's other creatures, and we are not in a position to pass judgment on the God who made them and us. It is also true that God led Job to repentance and forgiveness in part through his suffering.

> People don't reject God because of evil outside of themselves. They reject God because of their own evil, pride being paramount.

---

106 It is also true that in Job's attempt to understand why he is suffering as he is, he vacillates somewhat between trusting God and believing Him to be unjust.

QUESTION 6: DOES GOD USE OUR SUFFERING FOR HIS PURPOSES AND OUR GOOD?

Why did God allow Job to be afflicted the way he was? We can answer that question only in part in that we can see that God refined Job with fire; God made Job into a better person than he was before his suffering, possessing far more knowledge, wisdom, and understanding than he had before. (A little humility didn't hurt Job either.)

The same is true for the suffering God's people experience today. Romans 8:28 says, "And we know that for those who love God all things work together for good, for those who are called according to His purpose." That is God's promise to us, and when He says "all things," He means just that; He means that He will see to it that everything that happens to us, including the pain and suffering we endure, will work to our benefit. God may refine us with fire too, just as He did with Job—to better equip us to be His servants.

God's message to us is the same as His message to Job: "You need to trust Me. You may think you know better, but you don't. Just trust Me." And to all His people who suffer, through Paul, He said,

> No, in all these things we are more than conquerors through Him who loved us. For I am sure that neither death nor life, nor angels nor rulers, nor things present nor things to come, nor powers, nor height nor depth, nor anything else in all creation, will be able to separate us from the love of God in Christ Jesus our Lord. (Romans 8:37–39)

Job understood this, and as the backdrop to all his suffering and questioning, Job stood on the following confession, as stated by him:

> For I know that my Redeemer lives,
>   and at the last He will stand upon the earth.
> And after my skin has been thus destroyed,
>   yet in my flesh I shall see God,
>   whom I shall see for myself,
>   and my eyes shall behold, and not another.
>   My heart faints within me! (Job 19:25–27)

Yes, God's people experience grief, pain, and suffering, but we do so trusting Him—trusting that all our suffering will be used for that which is good and knowing that we await the final chapter in human history, which John described as follows:

And I heard a loud voice from the throne saying, "Behold, the dwelling place of God is with man. He will dwell with them, and they will be His people, and God Himself will be with them as their God. He will wipe away every tear from their eyes, and death shall be no more, neither shall there be mourning, nor crying, nor pain anymore, for the former things have passed away."
And He who was seated on the throne said, "Behold, I am making all things new." Also He said, "Write this down, for these words are trustworthy and true." (Revelation 21:3–5)

Some will ask, Why doesn't God do something about suffering and evil? We say, He has. He sent His Son, Jesus, to live and die on the cross for us so that our sins could be forgiven and we could live in fellowship with Him now and spend eternity with Him in heaven.

QUESTION 7: WHY DID GOD CREATE A WORLD THAT HE KNEW WOULD TURN TO EVIL?

We have, however, one final question to ask: If God knew that Adam and Eve would disobey Him and bring evil into the world, as they did, why did He create them? God could have simply chosen not to do it. In answer, we have to admit that we really don't understand why. His Word doesn't answer that question for us. We do know, however, as John 3:16 states, "For God so loved the world, that He gave His only Son, that whoever believes in Him should not perish but have eternal life." God loves us so much that He gave His Son to die on the cross for us so that we could be forgiven and could receive Him as Savior and Lord, united with Him as a bride is united to her beloved in marriage; so that we could live with Him, face-to-face in His presence, for all eternity.

When God created us, He could see the future. He knew we would disobey Him. When God created us, He could see David, His chosen king of Israel, murdering a good man in order to take the widow to be his wife. When God created us, He could see Peter cursing and swearing that he did not know Jesus, God's own Son. When God created us, He could see His Son hanging on the cross and crying out, "'Eli, Eli, lema sabachthani?' that is, 'My God, My God, why have You forsaken Me?'" (Matthew 27:46). When God created us, He knew who we would be and what we would do. He knew the pain and suffering we would bring upon one another—and upon Him—and yet, He created us anyway. Do we know why God created us in view of all this? We do not. We do know that He loves us so much that He gave up His Son for us on the cross. We know that by creating us, God was willing to pay an unimaginable

> God values us so much that He was willing to pay that price. If He wanted us to know more than that, He would have told us.

price. And He created us anyway. God values us so much that He was willing to pay that price. If He wanted us to know more than that, He would have told us. Jesus opened the door of paradise for us when He said on the cross, "It is finished." What more do we need to know?

QUESTIONS FOR REVIEW AND DISCUSSION

1. Jesus referred to His Church as His Bride. What does that say about the way He sees us?

2. What is the greatest act of love?

CHAPTER 13

THE PROBLEM OF DARWINISM

It is common for people to believe that Darwinian evolution disproves the historical accuracy of Genesis, the first book of the Bible. The views of the American public on this matter were summarized by a Gallup Poll conducted in 2014. Gallup found that 42 percent of Americans believe that God created the world in pretty much its current form and did so within the last ten thousand years or so. The poll also found that 31 percent of the public believes in theistic evolution, while 19 percent of those polled believe in atheistic evolution (Darwinism).[107]

This chapter will evaluate the arguments presented for evolution and against special creation as stated by Bill Nye in his debate with Ken Ham on February 4, 2014. We would expect that Mr. Nye presented what he believed were the strongest arguments in support of evolution. Because the debate was widely publicized, we would also expect that Nye was advised by other evolutionists as to how he should present the best case possible for his position. In this way, we have allowed the evolutionists themselves to identify what they apparently believe are their most convincing arguments. During the debate, Nye raised three objections to the Genesis account of creation. Interestingly, all of Nye's objections to Genesis focused on the age of the earth. Nye apparently believes that this is where Genesis is the most vulnerable. All three of the arguments he presented alleged that modern science has shown the earth to be much older than Genesis allows, and for that reason Genesis cannot be accurate history.[108]

Regarding the time of creation, we should note that Wisconsin Lutheran Seminary Professor John Brug gave a range for dating creation at six

---

107 Newport, "Human Origins."
108 "Transcript of Ken Ham vs. Bill Nye Debate," February 4, 2014, transcript by Bill Browning, February 10, 2014, Rocky Mountain Creation Fellowship, www.youngearth.org/index.php/archives/rmcf-articles/item/21-transcript-of-ken-ham-vs-bill-nye-debate.

thousand to twelve thousand years ago as being consistent with the biblical picture of creation. Hundreds of thousands or even many millions of years is not consistent with Genesis, said Brug.[109]

We now evaluate each of Nye's three arguments in turn.

ARGUMENT 1: ICE-CORE DATING

In his first argument, Nye said that the Greenland and Antarctic ice caps are known to be 680,000 or more years of age—far too old for Genesis to be accurate. Specifically, for instance, Nye said that ice-core dating methods have demonstrated that the Greenland ice cap is 680,000 years old. Mr. Nye actually made this assertion twice in the debate—suggesting that he believed it was a particularly strong argument, and that it exposed a major weakness in the creationist position.

Was Bill Nye correct in this matter? Can we assume the validity of his assumption that ice cores can be dated like tree rings with each ring representing a year in time? Do these ice cores prove that the Greenland ice is 680,000 years old? And are ice cores really verifiable scientific evidence against Genesis and for evolution?

We begin with the ice cap on Greenland. We can easily demonstrate that Bill Nye's alleged dates for the Greenland ice cap are totally false—and we can demonstrate they are false based on the recovery of an airplane called *Glacier Girl* in 1992. During World War II, on July 15, 1942, *Glacier Girl*'s squadron was forced to make an emergency landing on the Greenland ice cap. All the crew members were rescued, but *Glacier Girl*, along with the unit's five other P-38 fighters and two B-17 bombers, was abandoned and eventually buried beneath 264 feet of ice.[110] In 1992, the plane was discovered and brought to the surface by members of the Greenland Expedition Society. It was discovered after years of searching by several different parties. The aircraft was then restored to flying condition.

Numerous search parties had attempted to locate and rescue one of these planes but had failed. Why? An important reason is that the world of science had advised the would-be rescuers that the plane should have been, at most, forty feet below the surface of the ice, and probably far less than that. It turned out, however, that supposed maximum depth of forty feet was one-sixth of its actual depth.

---

109 Brug, "The Origins of Earth and People," 32.
110 "Glacier Girl: The Back Story," *Air & Space Magazine*, July 2007, www.airspacemag.com/history-of-flight/glacier-girl-the-back-story-19218360/?page=4.

***GLACIER GIRL* FLIES AGAIN.**
Wikimedia Commons, *The Glacier Girl* (November 6, 2006).

This means that we now know the actual rate of ice accumulation on Greenland. The plane did not sink in the ice. Doing so would have broken off its wings. All 264 feet of ice accumulated over the plane after it had been abandoned. The actual depth of the plane means that the scientific consensus regarding the rate of ice build-up on Greenland is wrong—so wrong that it should not be taken seriously. At the known rate of ice build-up on Greenland, as revealed by *Glacier Girl*, it would take about one thousand years to accumulate a mile-thick ice cap, which is what we now have. This information is consistent with reliable historical records revealing that Greenland was much warmer one thousand years ago than it is today and that, because of the favorable climate, some five thousand Norwegian settlers lived in Greenland at that time. There were two Norwegian colonies there. They were successful until the climate started getting cold around AD 1200. The agricultural colony came to an end in about AD 1400, and the fishing colony ceased to exist around 1450.[111]

Even if we allow for compaction of the deepest layers of ice on Greenland,

---

111 Eli Kintisch, "Why Did Greenland's Vikings Disappear?" *Science*, November 10, 2016, doi:10.1126/science.aal0363. For more on the history of Greenland's climate, see "Greenland: What Happened to the Greenland Norse?" (http://naturalhistory.si.edu/vikings/voyage/htmlonly/greenland.html; accessed July 6, 2017) as well as "The Fate of Greenland's Vikings," Dale Mackenzie Brown, *Archeology Archive*, February 28, 2000 (http://archive.archaeology.org/online/features/greenland/).

the entire ice cap easily could have accumulated during the biblical time frame as described in Genesis. The supposed 680,000-year-old age of the ice cap has been proven false. This means that an important argument used to discredit Genesis is now known to be mistaken. It also means that the assumption that ice cores can be dated like tree rings has been demonstrated to be false.

Why, then, would Bill Nye use an argument that is so easily discredited? There are several possible explanations. One may be that his worldview prevented him from seeing the obvious. Another possibility could be the assumption that the other scientists he had teamed up with couldn't possibly be wrong. Social scientists refer to this phenomenon as "group think," the process of blindly adopting the consensus of a group without ever examining its truthfulness.

Is the ice-core dating system used on Antarctica any more accurate than the one used on Greenland? No. It is the same fallacious system, and we now have trustworthy historical artifacts which reveal that the ice-core dating methods used for Antarctica, like those used for Greenland, are totally inaccurate. One such artifact is the map of Antarctica and other continents drawn in 1531 by French cartographer (mapmaker) Oronteus Finaeus. (This map can be seen by doing an Internet image search for the "Oronteus Finaeus map.")

First, the map pictures the globe from the perspective of the South Pole and shows Antarctica in the center. South America is pictured in the lower right, Africa and Madagascar in the lower left, and Australia in the upper left. There are numerous sensational features of the map—one of them being that it obviously pictures Antarctica as being largely ice-free and does so long before the continent was supposedly discovered in 1820. Second, the depiction of Antarctica is extraordinarily accurate—so accurate that modern mapmakers are mystified as to how it could have been drawn with such amazing precision. Obviously, the mapmaking ability of earlier people (perhaps the Phoenicians), including their abilities in mathematics and geometry, was far superior to what has been imagined by modern man.

The map not only shows much of Antarctica as being largely ice-free, it also pictures the coast of Antarctica in great detail, along with accurate depictions of major bays, rivers, and mountain ranges. This means that the evolutionary view that Antarctica has been covered with a mile-thick ice cap for 680,000 or more years is proven false. The dating system of the evolutionists is so far off that it is meaningless.

It should be noted that the authenticity of this map is essentially beyond question. Its author, Oronteus Finaeus, is a well-known figure of French history, having been chairman of the Department of Mathematics at College de France (1531–55) and having published numerous scholarly works under his own name—including this particular map. Finaeus would have used source maps to make his map. Another mapmaker of that era, Piri Reis, said that his source maps included those in use at the time of Alexander the Great (d. 325 BC). Based on his source maps and using his mathematical expertise, Finaeus drew this map of Antarctica. Finaeus, it should be added, calculated the value of pi to be 3.1410, a figure known to be quite accurate. Finaeus was a brilliant mathematician and cartographer.

There are other ancient maps that show Antarctica ice-free or at least largely ice-free.[112] One of them is the above-mentioned Piri Reis map of 1513. This map is also universally recognized as authentic. As noted above, Piri Reis said that his source maps dated back to the time of Alexander the Great.[113] Reis, like Finaeus, was an accomplished mathematician and cartographer.

It should also be mentioned that modern cartographers are amazed at the accuracy of these ancient maps. The navigational, mathematical, and mapmaking abilities of early people groups have been badly underestimated. The sophistication of these maps speaks for itself. I once gave a PowerPoint presentation relating to the age of the earth to an audience of high school teachers. After my speech, a man came up to me and said, "I hold a PhD in geography with emphasis in cartography, and you have opened up a whole new world for me." His education had ignored these maps.

The notion that Antarctica has been covered with a mile-thick ice cap for 680,000 or more years is proven false. The thesis that ice cores prove Genesis wrong is discredited, and it was one of Nye's primary objections to the historical accuracy of Genesis. It is significant to note that evolutionists use the same assumptions in dating the ice caps on Greenland and Antarctica. When the assumptions are proven false in both cases, the conclusion is very well established that the methodology of the evolutionists is faulty.

The position of the evolutionists reminds us of the reaction of the Jewish leaders to the frantic message given them by the soldiers who had been posted at Jesus' tomb. The guard unit told these leaders that an angel had

---

112 The Mercator World Map of 1538 also shows the Antarctic and its coastline in great detail, and the Bauche Map of 1737 shows Antarctica consisting of two land masses, something unknown to modern cartographers until it was revealed by sonograms in the early 1950s. The Hadji Ahmed Map of 1559 also shows Antarctica as well as a land bridge from Siberia to Alaska.

113 Jupp, "Piri Reis Map of Antarctica."

come and rolled away the stone, and the tomb was empty. The rational response would have been for the Jewish leaders to realize they had been wrong—that Jesus must be the Messiah after all. Why didn't they do so? Why did they adopt an irrational response instead of the response to which the evidence directed them? The reason is their minds were closed to the truth, and human nature is no different today.

ARGUMENT 2: OLD TJIKKO

The second objection to the creation account in Genesis focuses on a famous spruce tree—a Norway spruce called "Old Tjikko" that stands on a mountaintop in Sweden. (Lief Kullman, the man who discovered the tree, named it after his late dog, Tjikko.) In the debate, Nye said this tree is 9,550 years old.[114]

The audience attending the debate likely expected the age of this Swedish tree to have been determined in a reliable and verifiable manner, such as by counting growth rings. Not so. Nye didn't mention how the supposed age of the tree had been calculated at 9,550 years. He forgot to mention that the tree in question, according to an article in *National Geographic*, is 600 years old at most.[115] Six hundred years is a far cry from the 9,550 years Bill Nye claimed.

So where does this 9,550-year-old date come from? It was supposedly calculated by means of carbon 14 dating methods that were used on tree roots found underneath the tree. The argument is that the above-ground portion of the tree has died off numerous times, but the roots stayed alive and sent up new shoots to become new trees. That theory in and of itself raises serious questions about the dating methods used on this tree, but the real reason this argument raises serious questions is because carbon dating can only be used on plant and animal matter after it has died.

This leads us to ask, could dead Norway spruce roots survive for more than 9,550 years in moist soil without rotting away?[116] I happen to have a number of Norway spruce trees on my property in southern Minnesota. These trees belong to the same variety of spruce represented by Old Tjikko. One of these trees died about fifty years ago, and the stump was left in the ground. In order to determine the status of the roots of this tree after it had

---

114   Transcript of the Ken Ham vs Bill Nye Debate. See above, page 133, note 108.
115   Owen, "Oldest Living Tree."
116   Even if the dating method used here was accurate, which it is not, such methods cannot provide an accurate date with this specificity. It could supply a date of something like 9,500 years, plus or minus 200 years. The alleged date of 9,550 years is intended to mislead the public by suggesting a level of accuracy that carbon dating is incapable of providing.

been dead for fifty years, I draped a log chain over the stump, hooked the chain to a tractor and gave the stump a tug. As I expected, the spruce stump rolled out of the ground. The roots had rotted away, leaving the stump without an anchor to hold it place.

NORWAY SPRUCE TREES IN SOUTHERN MINNESOTA.

It is easily observed, therefore, that dead Norway spruce roots naturally rot away in something like fifty years, as can been seen from the rotted roots on the Norway spruce described above. How could roots from Old Tjikko survive nearly two hundred times that long? Such a claim is simply unbelievable. It appears that the argument is totally made up. We now commonly hear of "fake news." When it comes to Darwinism, we are largely dealing with fake evidence.

DO PEOPLE REALLY MAKE UP EVIDENCE?

Would those who wish to discredit the truth of the Bible simply make up their evidence? It does appear that this is the case. One of Darwin's foremost apologists, Ernst Haeckel, presented the now-famous drawings of various embryos to supposedly demonstrate that organisms retrace evolution in their embryonic development, and thereby prove evolution.

HAECKEL'S EMBRYOS.
Wikimedia Commons, "Haeckel drawings" (1892); public domain.

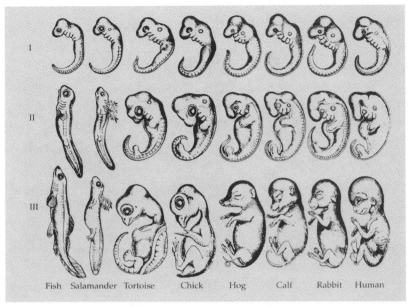

As mentioned above, Haeckel's drawings are intended to show that all embryos start out basically the same, and as they develop, they retrace evolutionary history up to their particular species (called *recapitulation*). Actual photographs of the organisms in Haeckel's drawings, however, have shown that the embryos are actually very different from one another. They are so different that well-respected British embryologist Michael Richardson, who examined Haeckel's drawings in great detail, concluded that these drawings were among the most famous fakes in biology.[117] Can we count on evolutionists to give accurate information about the supposed evidence for the theory? We cannot, and this reality must be kept in mind as we evaluate what the evolutionists say. We should also recognize that many biology textbooks still include these embryos as supposed proof for evolution even though they are known to be false. Noted embryologist Jonathan Wells has emphasized that the public is consistently being misled about the actual evidence for evolution. In evaluating the supposed evidence presented by Bill Nye in his

---

117 Richardson et. al., *Anatomy & Embryology*, 91–106.

debate with Ken Ham, the inaccurate use of evidence is clearly evident.[118]

It should be added that scientists at the time of Ernst Haeckel (1834–1919) knew very little about genetics. The modern science of genetics has demonstrated that Haeckel's thesis is wrong regardless of his faked drawings. Haeckel was trying to prove that every embryo, as it develops, retraces evolution. For this reason, the drawings are evidence for evolution, said Haeckel. From our present knowledge about genetics, however, we know that position to be false. A fertilized human egg contains the genetic information of a human being, nothing more and nothing less. That genetic information doesn't change as the person develops. A fertilized chicken egg contains the genetic information of a chicken. That organism will be nothing but a chicken throughout its life. The genetic information in a fertilized human is radically different from that in a fertilized chicken egg—this we know to be true. This genetic information does not change, and in the development of any organism, genetics is everything. For this reason, Haeckel's thesis that every organism retraces evolution is not only false, it is totally ridiculous. Yet, even that doesn't stop many evolutionists from using it as supposed evidence for evolution.

The public is consistently being misled about the actual evidence for evolution.

ARGUMENT 3: THE FOSSIL RECORD

The third argument Bill Nye used in his attempt to discredit Genesis was based on the fossil record. This record, said Nye, indicates that the earth is much older than Genesis allows it to be. But is this fossil history as typically pictured in biology textbooks accurate? It is not. For example, an important marker in the fossil record is that dinosaurs supposedly became extinct some sixty-five million years ago. Is that a reasonable date for the demise of dinosaurs? No. Another date used by some is that humans supposedly arrived on the scene one million years ago. Others go back two million years. Are those reasonable dates? They are not.[119]

---

118 Wells, *Icons of Evolution*, xii.
119 The date for the supposed arrival of humans is not agreed upon by scientists and the proposed date ranges have changed a number of times over the past few years. There are claims humans first arrived 200,000 years ago ("History of Life on Earth," *BBC earth*, www.bbc.co.uk/nature/history_of_the_earth, last updated October 2014), while others state that humans go back 400,000 years ("Human evolution," *Science Clarified*, accessed July 7, 2017, www.scienceclarified.com/He-In/Human-Evolution.html). Still others claim humans migrated out of Africa between 2 million and 1.8 million years ago ("Introduction to Human Evolution," Smithsonian National Museum of Natural History, last updated May 24, 2017, http://humanorigins.si.edu/education/introduction-human-evolution)

The question for us here is this: Did sixty-four million years separate dinosaurs and human beings as the evolutionists claim? What if it could be demonstrated that humans and dinosaurs actually lived at the same time? How much credibility would this geological argument then have? The entire geological timetable and sequences would be discredited.

In evaluating the fossil record, we need to recognize that both science and history have a major bearing on the question of the history of life on earth. For this reason, neglecting the relevant historical artifacts and written documents is contrary to what should be acceptable in professional research, and since all dating methods are based on assumptions that cannot be verified,[120] it's the genuine artifacts and documents that should carry the most weight on this issue. Verifiable historical documents and artifacts should take priority over assumptions every time.

We will begin our examination of the alleged sixty-four million year gap between dinosaurs and humans by observing that we now possess numerous ancient artworks that clearly depict dinosaurs. Some of these are engraved in stone, others are mosaics, and still others are sculptures. In many cases, even the actual species of the dinosaurs can be identified. These pieces of art are that explicit. For example, on a wall in an ancient temple in Cambodia, there is a carved-in-stone relief of a stegosaurus.[121] (Other examples can be searching the Internet for "ancient artworks of dinosaurs.")[122]

The authenticity of many of these works of art is virtually beyond question. The only reasonable conclusion is that people and dinosaurs lived at the same time. Perhaps not all artists saw the dinosaurs themselves, but if they didn't have firsthand knowledge of dinosaurs, they must have had access to other artworks or reports of some kind that allowed them to construct their art with such amazing accuracy.

These examples and others like them raise serious questions about the validity of the geological column and related timetables used by evolutionists. It is actually more than that—these historical artifacts leave the geological timetable in shambles.

---

120 All dating methods assume certain characteristics of the substance being dated at the beginning of the aging process. These assumptions are just guesses except in the case of carbon 14, where the assumptions match observable processes. Carbon 14, however, is useful for only a few thousand years and could have been distorted by any number of cataclysmic events.

121 This carving and similar artworks can be seen at "Ancient Dinosaur Depictions," Genesis Park, www.genesispark.com/exhibits/evidence/historical/ancient/dinosaur/ (accessed July 6, 2017).

122 See also *Ten Truths about Evolution That Everyone Should Know* (Allen Quist, 2014), available at Lutheran Synod Book Company, 700 Luther Drive, Mankato, MN, 56001. Also available online at els.org/our-work-together/dc-2.

It should also be mentioned that evolutionary scientists are now admitting that soft tissue is frequently found in dinosaur bones.[123] The world of science has said for years that soft tissue could not survive beyond a few thousand years at most. It has taken a few years for evolutionists to make the admission that, yes, some dinosaur bones contain soft tissue. The existence of this soft tissue is beyond dispute because it can be seen under a microscope. Does this mean the evolutionists are willing to reconsider their position that dinosaurs have been extinct for sixty-five million years? Not at all. They are now looking for an explanation for how soft tissue could have survived that long. At this time, they have no demonstrable answers. They do have theoretical explanations, but the matter is really a mystery for them. At the same time, evolutionists commonly say that their views are substantiated, in part, because evolution is successful in making predictions—a position that is yet to be verified. With soft tissue, at minimum, we have a major discovery that runs contrary to their prediction—that dinosaur bones could not contain soft tissue.

This current position of the evolutionists reminds us of the story of a psychologist who was treating a patient who was convinced he was dead. In an attempt to change the patient's mind, the psychologist took him to a morgue. The psychologist rolled out several bodies from the refrigeration where they were stored and proceeded to stick each with a pin. After each pin prick, the psychologist said to his patient, "Look, no blood." After the patient agreed that dead people do not bleed, the psychologist pricked him with a pin. A large drop of deep red blood formed quickly at the spot of injury. And how did the patient respond? He exclaimed: "My stars, dead people bleed after all!"

In addition to the artwork of dinosaurs and the discovery of soft tissue in their bones, we also have written records that may depict dinosaurs and other creatures that were their contemporaries. Job 40 contains one such account:

>Behold, Behemoth,
>>which I made as I made you;
>>he eats grass like an ox.
>Behold, his strength in his loins,
>>and his power in the muscles of his belly.
>He makes his tail stiff like a cedar;
>>the sinews of his thighs are knit together.
>His bones are tubes of bronze,

---

123 Fields, "Dinosaur Shocker."

> his limbs like bars of iron.
> He is the first of the works of God;
> > let Him who made him bring near His sword!
> For the mountains yield food for him
> > where all the wild beasts play.
> Under the lotus plants he lies,
> > in the shelter of the reeds and in the marsh.
> For his shade the lotus trees cover him;
> > the willows of the brook surround him.
> Behold, if the river is turbulent he is not frightened;
> > he is confident though Jordan rushes against
> > his mouth.
> Can one take him by his eyes,
> > or pierce his nose with a snare? (vv. 15–24)

What is this animal? Some scholars have suggested that it is an elephant; others say that it could be a hippopotamus. Christian apologetics organization Answers in Genesis, however, believes that this animal could be a large dinosaur.[124] The description does appear to fit a large sauropod dinosaur very well. A sauropod dinosaur was an herbivorous (plant-eating) land-dwelling animal that can accurately be identified as the first rank (largest) of the land-dwelling creatures made by God. A sauropod also had a tail like a cedar tree; elephants and hippos do not. The creature's name, behemoth, is a Hebrew word for "megabeast"—which also fits a sauropod very well.

The translators of the King James Version of the Bible (1604–11) did not know what this creature was, so they transliterated (spelled) the Hebrew word תומהב (behemoth) into English. Recent translations have generally followed suit. There is no agreement among Bible scholars regarding the identity of this creature, so you, the reader, will have to decide for yourself. Scholars generally treat the creature as a real animal, not as a mythological being. The question to ask, then, is: What animal, past or present, best fits the description of Behemoth? I recently received an email from a pastor who explained that he had been giving instruction to a young woman who wished to be baptized. He wrote the following:

> I am taking her through instruction with hopes that she will be baptized at the end of November. Today she came with questions about dinosaurs existing prior to humans; she was very perplexed

---

124 Driver, "Sea Monsters."

by this, saying this had always bothered her about whether the Bible was true or not.

I used some of your talk and your photos of ancient artwork depicting these creatures along with human beings. It completely took away her doubts, and we had a nice conversation looking at the texts in the Book of Job.[125]

This account about one pastor's experience in adult instruction reveals that it is important for people to know that the evolutionary view of history is far from proven fact. Too many people have been led to believe that evolution has proven the historical account in the Bible to be false. They need to realize that there is an important and persuasive other side to this issue.

The next creature described in Job is also of great interest to us:

> Can you draw out Leviathan with a fishhook
> or press down his tongue with a cord?
> Can you put a rope in his nose
> or pierce his jaw with a hook?
> Will he make many pleas to you?
> Will he speak to you soft words?
> Will he make a covenant with you
> to take him for your servant forever?
> Will you play with him as with a bird,
> or will you put him on a leash for your girls?
> Will traders bargain over him?
> Will they divide him up among the merchants?
> Can you fill his skin with harpoons
> or his head with fishing spears?
> Lay your hands on him;
> remember the battle—you will not do it again!
> Behold, the hope of a man is false;
> he is laid low even at the sight of him.
> No one is so fierce that he dares to stir him up.
> Who then is he who can stand before Me?
> Who has first given to Me, that I should repay him?
> Whatever is under the whole heaven is Mine.
>
> I will not keep silence concerning his limbs,
> or his mighty strength, or his goodly frame.

---

[125] I received this email in 2015; names are withheld to protect privacy. Reprinted by permission.

Who can strip off his outer garment?
    Who would come near him with a bridle?
Who can open the doors of his face?
    Around his teeth is terror.
His back is made of rows of shields,
    shut up closely as with a seal.
One is so near to another
    that no air can come between them.
They are joined one to another;
    they clasp each other and cannot be separated.
His sneezings flash forth light,
    and his eyes are like the eyelids of the dawn.
Out of his mouth go flaming torches;
    sparks of fire leap forth.
Out of his nostrils comes forth smoke,
    as from a boiling pot and burning rushes.
His breath kindles coals,
    and a flame comes forth from his mouth.
In his neck abides strength,
    and terror dances before him.
The folds of his flesh stick together,
    firmly cast on him and immovable.
His heart is hard as a stone,
    hard as the lower millstone.
When he raises himself up, the mighty are afraid;
    at the crashing they are beside themselves.
Though the sword reaches him, it does not avail,
    nor the spear, the dart, or the javelin.
He counts iron as straw,
    and bronze as rotten wood.
The arrow cannot make him flee;
    for him, sling stones are turned to stubble.
Clubs are counted as stubble;
    he laughs at the rattle of javelins.
His underparts are like sharp potsherds;
    he spreads himself like a threshing sledge on the mire.
He makes the deep boil like a pot;
    he makes the sea like a pot of ointment.
Behind him he leaves a shining wake;
    one would think the deep to be white-haired.

> On earth there is not his like,
> a creature without fear.
> He sees everything that is high;
> he is king over all the sons of pride. (Job 41)

Up until a few years ago, this creature was commonly identified as a Nile crocodile. Some individuals, in contrast, thought it was a sea monster of some kind. In 1997, however, a half-complete skeleton of SuperCroc (*Sarcosuchus imperator*) was unearthed in a dry river bed in the Sahara Desert. From this skeleton and other skeletons of the same species but less complete, we know what this creature was like. We now know that SuperCroc was similar to today's largest crocodiles, but it was ten times larger! It weighed in at ten tons[126]—making it much bigger than Tyrannosaurus rex (five and one-half to seven and three-quarters tons).[127]

The description in Job 41 appears to be a good match for SuperCroc. Some people question the fire-breathing imagery, but that could be figurative language, similar to the "bones of brass" metaphor used to describe Behemoth in Job 40. Notice, also, the similarity of the fire-breathing imagery in Job and in the description of God's anger in 2 Samuel 22:9: "Smoke went up from His nostrils, and devouring fire from His mouth; glowing coals flamed forth from Him." This description of God's anger in 2 Samuel is obviously figurative; the fire-breathing depiction of the Leviathan in Job 41 could be as well. Following are some of the striking points of similarity between Leviathan and SuperCroc:

1. The Hebrew word *leviathan* means "one who twists." Members of the crocodilian family are well-known for their ability to rip their prey apart by locking their jaws unto a portion of their prey's body and then commencing with a violent twisting action that tears the prey apart. This is known as the crocodile's death roll.
2. Leviathan is described in Job as having a very strong neck. All crocodilians do have extremely muscular necks. In addition, crocodilians have the ability to lock the vertebrae of their necks together so that no twisting in their neck is possible. As a result, the full impact of the death roll is transmitted to their hapless prey.
3. Leviathan's back is described as follows:

    > His back is made of rows of shields,

---
126 Sereno, "SuperCroc."
127 American Museum, "The Problem of Size."

> shut up closely as with a seal.
> One is so near to another
> > that no air can come between them.
> They are joined one to another;
> > they clasp each other and cannot be separated.
> (Job 41:15–17)

Job 42 additionally states that no arrow or spear can penetrate this body armor of Leviathan. SuperCroc's back and neck were covered with bony shields called *scutes*. They overlapped like the siding on a house so that no spear or arrow could penetrate to the vital organs of this massive crocodile. No other creature, past or present, has body armor anything like this.

4. Leviathan's underside is described as being covered with pieces of broken pottery—a vivid description of the body armor on the belly of SuperCroc.
5. Leviathan was at home in the water and also on land, as is the case with all crocodilians.
6. In the summation of Leviathan's characteristics, God says he is "king" of the creatures He has made, and that nothing on earth is his equal—a good fit for SuperCroc. Even its scientific name, *Sarcosuchus imperator,* fits Leviathan in that *imperator* is Latin for "king." In comparing him to a Tyrannosaurus rex, as mentioned, SuperCroc was almost twice as big. He also had a bite that was twice as strong, possessed extraordinary body armor of which T. rex had none, and could drag his opposition into the water and drown it. T. rex was no match for SuperCroc, who was, indeed, king of all the land animals God had made.

As we have seen, therefore, Leviathan and SuperCroc are a good match. But wait, SuperCroc and the other huge crocodiles were thought to be contemporaries of the dinosaurs. He was said to have eaten dinosaurs for lunch. Evolutionists say SuperCroc became extinct even before the dinosaurs—100 million years ago. So how could Job have known what he was like? How could Job have known what he was like in such extraordinary detail? If Leviathan is SuperCroc, then Job had seen him—or had received very detailed accounts from other people who had seen him.

As far as biblical scholarship is concerned, this information is relatively new. SuperCroc does fit the description of Leviathan extremely well. Identifying a Nile crocodile with Leviathan is not out of the question, however. As time goes on, it will be fascinating to see how biblical scholarship responds to this relatively new information. Meanwhile, the Darwinian history of life is further called into question. And it's time that somebody informed the public about it.[128]

QUESTIONS FOR REVIEW AND DISCUSSION

1. Additional artworks of ancient peoples that picture dinosaurs are being discovered even today. There are at least fifty such works of art now available. The mainstream media seems to ignore these discoveries for the most part. In contrast, every so often a new "missing link" in the history of man is discovered, only to be dismissed as a false lead a few years later. How can this double-standard be explained?

2. As mentioned earlier, John Sanford's work demonstrates that natural selection cannot substantially improve a living kind, nor can it bring about new kinds. Why might secular science want to ignore what he says?

---

128 For an in-depth evaluation of the evidence supporting evolution, see Jonathan Wells's book *Icons of Evolution*.

PART 4

DEFENDING THE
MORAL LAW

CHAPTER 14

NATURAL LAW

Up to this point, we have focused on the reasons for recognizing the truthfulness of the Christian Gospel message. The apostle Paul, however, said, "I did not shrink from declaring to you the *whole counsel of God*" (Acts 20:27, emphasis added). The "whole counsel of God" consists of both the glorious Gospel that Jesus died for the sins of the entire world and His moral law. Do we have objective evidence for the reality of God's moral law as well as evidence for the truthfulness of His Gospel? Yes, we do. And how can we proclaim the Gospel message to those who deny the genuineness of the moral law and for that reason will see no need for the Gospel? We can do so by explaining and documenting the reality of the universal moral code. That is, we can do so by describing the nature and verifying the existence of natural law.

We have verified the reliability of the Scriptures, and they explain God's moral law in great detail. By verifying the Scriptures, therefore, we have also verified the reality of the moral law. This chapter will demonstrate that God's moral law has additionally been verified by recent scientific research.

Paul said in Romans that all persons reveal that "the work of the law is written on their hearts" (Romans 2:15). This innate understanding of God's moral law is what we know as natural law. There are two avenues by which we can understand God's moral law, God's moral expectations of us: one is by God's revelation to us in His Word (revealed law as illustrated by the Ten Commandments); the other is by God having implanted His moral law within us when He made us human beings (natural law). To be human is to possess the knowledge of God's moral law. Regardless of how we come to understand this moral law, whether by revelation or by nature, the essential content of the moral law is one and the same.

We have observed that Paul boldly proclaimed the moral law to the philosophers on Mars Hill, but he did so on the basis of natural law, not the Ten Commandments. Paul's pagan audience would have had little or no regard for the Ten Commandments, God's revealed law. Today, we may wish—or need—to make similar arguments. For that reason, this chapter will explore six fundamental principles of natural law, explain the scientific evidence for its characteristics and existence, and make suggestions on how understanding natural law can be useful in evangelism.

In Romans, Paul outlined the characteristics of natural law as follows:

> For when Gentiles, who do not have the law, by nature do what the law requires, they are a law to themselves, even though they do not have the law. They show that the work of the law is written on their hearts, while their conscience also bears witness, and their conflicting thoughts accuse or even excuse them. (2:14–15)

In this way, Paul clarified that the moral law has governed human behavior since the beginning of time. Paul also meant that the Ten Commandments provide considerable detail about the moral law, but the moral law is known to everyone by nature, by being human, and for that reason all people have always been aware of, and subject to, this moral law.

Martin Luther called Romans "the chief part of the New Testament,"[129] and it is apparent from this statement in Romans that natural law holds an important place in both Christian theology and apologetics. We will see that understanding natural law is especially important in the relativistic age in which we live.

Sadly, however, there is a dearth of contemporary materials on natural law. Reformed theologian J. Daryl Charles commented on a reason for this lack of good materials: "What is conspicuous to the theologian and moral philosopher is the disappearance of this conviction [that natural law is real and important] in modern Protestant thought."[130]

In marked contrast to the inadequate study of natural law today, Martin Luther and the other reformers displayed a clear and thoroughly biblical understanding, as well as appreciation, of natural law. This doesn't mean, however, that they devoted a large amount of time and attention to it. The reformers focused their speaking and writing largely on those issues where there was serious dispute. The reformers, for the most part, did not take issue with the Roman Church nor with one another on the existence of natural law, and consequently they said relatively little about it.

Natural law, however, is now denied by the most influential worldviews of Western culture. Whether we speak of secular humanism, postmodernism, materialism, or behaviorism—all of which have their roots in Darwinian

---

129   AE 35:365.
130   Charles, *Natural Law*, xiii.

evolution—the contemporary and nonbiblical ideologies of today typically reject all genuine morality, including natural law. Because the denial of morality is a logical conclusion resulting from the naturalistic assumptions of modern philosophies, a familiarity with the non-Christian worldviews to which we are all exposed every day will shed considerable light on the denial of natural law.

We have come a long way from Scholasticism and the Enlightenment, where natural law was recognized and valued. Today, natural law is commonly denied. Those who subscribe to natural law are often subjected to personal attacks, including being called "hateful" and "bigots." When Justice Clarence Thomas was appointed to the US Supreme Court in 1992, those who opposed his nomination did so primarily because of his adherence to natural law.[131] The reason for this opposition to Clarence Thomas was that relative morality ("right is what's right for you") cannot be defended if natural law exists. Relative morality is embraced and aggressively promoted in our schools, in the cinema, and all too often in our churches. The popularity of films such as *Fifty Shades of Grey* provides stark testimony to the grotesque perversion of the moral law in our time.

The need for accurate instruction on natural law is everywhere evident. Ask most any group of people this question: "How many of you believe morality is universal and absolute?" Not many will raise their hands. But ask, "Do you see right and wrong as being that which is right and wrong for you?" Most people in most groups will agree that such is the case. The dominant position of our culture is "Morality is a personal choice" and "Who are you to judge?" *Tolerance* is the God-word of our time. In the field of education, for instance, any distinction between *diversity, tolerance,* and *relative morality* is hazy at best and nonexistent at worst.

But to our relativistic world, Romans 2:14–15 speaks with clarity, truthfulness, and power. Romans speaks of the genuineness and importance of natural law, a reality that in our time is continually denied and vilified, but at the same time is easily observed and has actually now been substantiated by brilliant and repeatable scientific research. When Romans speaks of natural law, it describes an integral part of our nature as human beings—a part of our nature that is indispensable for civilized life and is arguably essential for the continuation of human life itself in that we would likely kill one another off without it. It speaks of a reality that enables mission work to be successful—even among those who, on the surface, deny its existence.

---

[131] This same drama was played out again, albeit to a lesser degree, with the appointment of Neil Gorsuch to the US Supreme Court in 2017.

SIX FUNDAMENTAL PRINCIPLES OF NATURAL LAW

We turn again to Romans 2:14–15 and allow Paul to enlighten us on natural law. Paul's exposition explains why everyone needs the Gospel message of Jesus Christ, but as we will see, Paul's description of natural law also embodies important insights that help equip us with workable methods for evangelism as well. Paul writes, "For when Gentiles, who do not have the law, by nature do what the law requires, they are a law to themselves, even though they do not have the law. They show that the work of the law is written on their hearts, while their conscience also bears witness, and their conflicting thoughts accuse or even excuse them."

As we will see, six fundamental principles of natural law are clearly stated in these two verses of Scripture.

WHAT IS NATURAL LAW?

Verse 14 above describes three principles of natural law: (1) Natural law is instinctive; (2) the moral code, including natural law, is singular and universal; and (3) natural law includes both tables of the Law.

1. Natural law is instinctive.

Paul said that the Gentiles—who do not have the revealed moral law, the Ten Commandments—nevertheless follow the principles of the moral law and do so "by nature." From this statement, we derive our theological term *natural law*.

It is commonly said that the precepts of natural law are known by logic. While that is partly true, Paul clarified in verse 15 that God's moral law has been "written on their hearts." Today, we would say the moral law is instinctive; it's part of the genetic code of human beings. We don't need to use logic to be aware of information that is instinctive; the knowledge is just there, though we may use logic to apply and better understand this instinctive knowledge.

Consider, for example, the intricate nest of a Baltimore oriole. It is woven together from grass or string or other material in a way that forms a warm and secure pouch within which the eggs are laid and the young are kept warm and secure until they fledge. The nest will be located on the slender outer branches of a tree, making it difficult for a predator to find or access. It will be anchored from three or more attachment points for its overall structure and stability and will be lined with soft insulating material, such as down or any cotton-like substance.

How did the orioles learn to make this marvelous nest? They never observed such a nest being built themselves. The answer, of course, is they didn't learn it. The knowledge to build the nest is written in their genetic code. The knowledge is instinctive.

BALTIMORE ORIOLES WITH NEST.
"Baltimore orioles and nest." iStockphoto.com.

Reasoning from the lesser to the greater, if God can put the knowledge of how to build this nest into the genetic code of an oriole, He can certainly put the innate knowledge of the moral law into human beings and do so at the moment of conception. In this chapter, we will evaluate whether He actually did so.

We marvel at the complexity of the DNA molecule that makes up the genetic structure of all life. At the same time, however, the DNA molecule only stores and transmits information. The most extraordinary thing is the information itself. In the case of a fertilized human egg, for instance, the knowledge contained in the genome of this single cell is the knowledge of how to construct a particular human being. (The genome is the sum total of all the genetic information of any organism.) The creation of a new life is primarily a matter of information, and the Creator God who put the information of how to build a human being into a small part of a single cell can easily include the knowledge of the moral law in that same cell. From the viewpoint of biology, everything that defines what it means to be human is in this single cell. We will see in this section that this is exactly what He did. This knowledge of the moral law is part of what Genesis meant by stating that we have been created in God's image, broadly defined.

2. Natural law is singular and universal.

Notice that Paul, even though he is speaking of both the revealed moral code and the natural law, is treating the moral law as being one singular entity. The content of all of them are one and the same. The Gentiles do not have a fundamentally different moral law from the Jews who have the revealed law. The content of the moral law, whether known by revelation or by instinct and logic, is one and the same.

This truth is essential to a proper understanding of natural law. There are not two moral codes, but only one. You can no more have more than one moral law than you can have more than one law of gravity. All laws of nature, be they moral or physical, are singular.

> You can no more have more than one moral law than you can have more than one law of gravity.

For this reason, it is highly misleading to speak of "Christian morality" or of "Judeo-Christian ethics." Such language implies that Christians have a moral code that is different from other people or groups. This is not true. You could just as well speak of "Christian gravity." Such talk stands in the way of proclaiming the whole counsel of God because it implies that morality is not an objective and changeless part of the world God created. It implies that morality is a product of a culture and, therefore, is not universally binding. If this were true, if morality is a mere construct of culture, there is then no need for a Savior. This language provides fodder for those who would deny natural law by saying, "Don't impose your moral values on me." There is no such thing as "your moral values," any more than there is "your law of gravity." Morality is not relative. It is not the possession of a particular person, culture, or religion. It is not self-chosen. Morality is not analogous to deciding which color socks to put on in the morning. Morality is universal and absolute. The moral code is not affected by the degree to which we recognize it, try to rationalize it away, or even attempt to deny it. The moral law is, and we are powerless to change it in any way.

In addition, postmodernism, the philosophy that truth and morality are determined by a particular culture, is given credibility by the language of "Christian values" or "Christian morality." This careless talk enables postmodernists and other relativists to feel comfortable with their false worldviews that deny genuine morality. We will hopefully want to challenge these relativists by showing them the reality of natural law and applying it to their lives, not enable them in their error and salve their conscience by misleading talk that allows them to feel comfortable about their state of being lost sinners.

No one understood the singularity and universality of the moral law better than Martin Luther. Luther emphasized this singularity and universality when he said, "Where he [Moses] gives commandment, we are not to follow him except so far as he agrees with natural law."[132] Meaning, the content of the natural law and the moral law are one and the same. But in addition, Luther recognized that to a limited degree the Ten Commandments include

---

132 AE 35:173.

the ceremonial law as well as the moral—the commandment to keep the Sabbath is ceremonial law—and that we are bound only by the moral law portions of the Ten Commandments, not the ceremonial law portion.

Luther later explained that the Ten Commandments are in complete agreement with the law of nature, and for that reason, all the people who lived before Moses had the moral code and have no excuse for having broken it. The Ten Commandments, however, provide us with far greater detail than does natural law, and for that reason the Commandments are easier to apply and more difficult to rationalize away. The Lutheran Confessions, like Luther, say that people understand the singular moral law by nature because it is written in the minds of all people.[133]

Even though the moral law has been there in the hearts of all people for all time, it must also be recognized that everyone has the propensity to distort it, rationalize it away, or in various ways deny it. Paul said in Romans 1:21, "They became futile in their thinking, and their foolish hearts were darkened." Luther described those who deny or distort the moral law by saying they are "like people who purposely stop their ears or pinch their eyes shut to close out sound and sight." But Luther added this clarification: "They do not succeed in this; their conscience tells them otherwise."[134]

We conclude, then, that all people have the knowledge of the singular and universal moral law of God. And even though this knowledge is darkened by sin, it is nevertheless still there, and it will have a significant impact on how people think and conduct their lives. The conscience can be seared; it cannot be eliminated.

3. Natural law includes both tables of the Law.

Natural law includes the existence of God and our responsibility to Him as well as our responsibility to one another. C. S. Lewis explained that if a moral law exists, then a Lawgiver must also exist; the two are necessarily interconnected.[135] Lewis used this observation in making the "moral argument" for the existence of God. As Lewis said, it can easily be observed that all people groups adhere to a moral code that has much more in common with the moral codes of other groups than it has differences. This universal moral code implies a Lawgiver. This Lawgiver is God.[136]

---

133 Apology of the Augsburg Confession, Article IV, paragraph 7, *Concordia: The Lutheran Confessions.*
134 AE 19:54.
135 Lewis, *Mere Christianity*, 37–39.
136 Lewis, *Mere Christianity*, 39.

The Lutheran Confessions say the same, acknowledging that even after the fall, there exists in all people a "dim spark" of the knowledge that there is a God, and also of the doctrine of the moral law that they have by nature.[137] This means that the natural knowledge of God is both instinctive and at the same time a logical conclusion based on observing the natural world. Paul said in Romans, "For His invisible attributes, namely, His eternal power and divine nature, have been clearly perceived, ever since the creation of the world in the things that have been made. So they are without excuse" (1:20).

We should not be surprised, then, that most people believe God exists. Earlier, we discussed a 2016 Gallup Poll where 89 percent of Americans answered yes to the question, "Do you believe in God?"[138] It should be noted, however, that 98 percent had said yes to the same question as recently as 1967.[139] It would appear that the ongoing indoctrination in Darwinism and relativism in our time is having an effect.

When the existence of God is denied, we once again see the connection between the law and Lawgiver. It was Dostoevsky's Ivan, the atheist, who said that if there is no God, then everything is permitted, everything is lawful. There are then no moral rules that we are obligated to obey.[140] Those who want no moral constraints on their lives are inclined to deny God's existence for that reason.

Nevertheless, as Luther said, the knowledge of God and His moral law is still there in all people.[141] In many cases, it can be accessed in preparation for their hearing the Good News of Jesus Christ.

THE SCIENTIFIC EVIDENCE FOR NATURAL LAW

We now turn to the second part of Paul's exposition on natural law, Romans 2:15: "They show that the work of the law is written on their hearts, while their conscience also bears witness, and their conflicting thoughts accuse or even excuse them." In this verse, we will observe the last three principles of natural law: (4) Natural law is observable; (5) therefore, natural law can be studied scientifically; and (6) our conscience testifies to the content and reality of natural law. As we will see, this is the part of Paul's discourse where science and theology intersect.

---

137 Solid Declaration of the Formula of Concord, Article II, paragraph 9, *Concordia: The Lutheran Confessions*.
138 Newport, "Most Americans."
139 Newport, "More Than 9 in 10 Americans."
140 Dostoevsky, *Brothers Karamazov*, 200. Note: Jean-Paul Sartre said essentially the same thing.
141 AE 19:54

4. Natural law is observable.

Paul said that those who have never learned the Ten Commandments still "show that the work of the law is written in their hearts" (Romans 2:15). In our daily lives, we can readily observe evidence of natural law in the minds of all people. For example, when we hear of murders, rapes, and terrorist acts on the evening news, how many of us view such acts as morally defensible? Do the newscasts put up some authority figure to say such actions are wrong? Or do they assume viewers will naturally reach that conclusion on their own? (There are exceptions, of course, such as some Muslims who have been indoctrinated into believing that terrorism is morally acceptable. Indoctrination can override one's understanding of natural law to a degree.)

When people conclude that such behavior is wrong, they are unconsciously appealing to a moral standard. The standard to which they appeal is not a standard just for Americans, nor just for themselves, nor just for Christians. They appeal to a universal standard of right versus wrong. That is the only way that "crimes against humanity" make sense. As noted above, a real standard of right versus wrong cannot exist in a world of nature plus nothing (materialism). No morality can be found in the fields of physics, chemistry, biology, and mathematics. That is, no morality can be found in a world of nature alone, a world that can be described by natural science alone. As Richard Dawkins said, a world without God is a world without genuine right and wrong.[142]

Recognition of genuine moral standards does not require references to the Ten Commandments, or the right to life or property, or any such written or commonly described standard. The standards are an inherent part of the worldview of the viewers. This is not to say that interpretation is never needed—it often is. But the point is simply this: everyone has the basic moral standards embedded in their minds, and they frequently reveal these standards in their daily lives by what they say and do.

Even in cases where people say they subscribe to some kind of relativistic morality, it can quickly be seen they don't actually believe it. For example, I once had a conversation with a pastor manning a Planned Parenthood booth. This pastor, obviously quite liberal in his thinking, began his pitch by saying that all morality is situational and relative.[143] I asked the pastor what he would think of someone approaching the woman sitting next to him, taking out a gun, and killing her on the spot. The pastor replied, "That would

---

[142] Dawkins, "Science and God," 892.
[143] Situational ethics was popularized in the mid- to late twentieth century by philosopher Joseph Fletcher.

be terrible." When asked why it would be terrible, he exclaimed, "Because that would be murder." When asked why murder was terrible, he declared, "Everyone knows murder is wrong!" The words had barely left his lips when he realized he had just contradicted his view that all morality is situational and relative. By saying that everyone knows murder is wrong, this man was appealing to a universal moral code; he was appealing to natural law—the existence of which he had just moments before denied.

C. S. Lewis described this same truth as follows:

> The most remarkable thing is this. Whenever you find a man who says he does not believe in a real Right and Wrong, you will find the same man going back on this a moment later. He may break his promise to you, but if you try breaking one to him he will be complaining "It's not fair" before you can say Jack Robinson.[144]

No one can function in a civilized society and follow relativistic morality. The humanists found that even they couldn't do so. Humanist Manifesto II (1973) said that morality is autonomous and situational, that it was not subject to any theological or ideological sanction.[145] By the time the humanists revised their belief statement in 1980, however, they had changed their minds and said that there are universal moral standards after all.[146] The moral standards specified by the humanists in 1980 leave much to be desired, but nevertheless, these standards demonstrate that even the humanists couldn't long defend their view that morality is strictly relative and self-chosen.

5. Because natural law is observable, it is subject to scientific evaluation and description.

Not many people who write on natural law appear to recognize that the reality of natural law has been scientifically verified. This verification has been repeated by various members of the scientific community and has been described in considerable detail in a number of peer-reviewed scientific journals and other publications.[147]

Going back to the words of Romans 2:15, Paul said, they "show that the

---

144 Lewis, *Mere Christianity*, 19. Copyright © C. S. Lewis Pte. Ltd. 1942, 1943, 1944, 1952. Extract reprinted by permission.
145 American Humanist Association, "Manifesto II."
146 See "A Secular Humanist Declaration," 1980, www.secularhumanism.org/index.php/11. This statement parrots the language of Lawrence Kohlberg, thereby strongly suggesting that his work was instrumental in the humanists being virtually forced to revise their views.
147 See Elliot Abramson, "Puncturing the Myth of the Moral Intractability of Law Students," *Notre Dame Journal of Law, Ethics & Public Policy*, vol. 7, issue 1, Symposium on Legal Ethics Article 7, February 2014.

work of the law is written in their hearts." That is, Paul said that the effects of natural law are observable. As mentioned above, this means that the effects of natural law are available for scientifically based description and verification.

We are speaking here primarily of the ground-breaking research of Dr. Lawrence Kohlberg (1927–87) of Harvard University. Kohlberg has commonly been described as one of the most influential scholars in the field of psychology in the twentieth century, and he has been consistently recognized as the world's foremost authority in the social sciences on the subject of morality.

Kohlberg's research focused on how people of different ages and from different cultures make moral decisions. His method was that of confronting people with moral dilemmas and asking for their solution to the dilemmas. He found many of these dilemmas in theological discussions of casuistry (the study of circumstances where moral values conflict). The most famous such dilemma is known as the Heinz dilemma and reads as follows:

> A woman was near death from a very bad disease, a special kind of cancer. There was one drug that the doctors thought might save her. It was a form of radium that a druggist in the same town had recently discovered. The drug was expensive to make, but the druggist was charging ten times what the drug cost him to make. He paid $200 for the radium and charged $2,000 for a small dose of the drug. The sick woman's husband, Heinz, went to everyone he knew to borrow the money, but he could only get together only about $1,000 which was half of what it cost. He told the druggist that his wife was dying and asked him to sell it cheaper or let him pay later. But the druggist said,: "No, I discovered the drug and I'm going to make money from it." Heinz got desperate and broke into the man's laboratory to steal the drug for his wife. Should Heinz have broken into the man's store to steal the drug for his wife?
>
> Should the husband have done that? Was it right or wrong?[148]

Kohlberg's interest in how people responded to the dilemmas did not focus primarily on their answer of yes or no, but rather on how they defended their answer. Kohlberg recognized that people could defend their solution to a moral conflict only by appealing to a moral standard of some kind.

One of Kohlberg's most important observations in using this methodology was that people from all cultures appeal to the same moral standards

---

[148] Kohlberg, "The Philosophy of Moral Development," 12.

in defense of their answers. That is, moral values are essentially the same in all cultures and nations throughout the world. Kohlberg also determined that people from various religions similarly hold to largely the same moral standards.

This means that morality is universal and absolute, not relative. It also means that Christianity is not unique with regard to moral standards, as we know, but rather is unique regarding how we can satisfy these standards.

Kohlberg additionally found that as people grow and mature, they pass through different stages of moral development. This is a prime example of scientific research not only confirming what the Bible says but also adding important details to what the Scriptures have stated.[149] Kohlberg determined there are six stages of moral development:

> *Stage one (avoid pain):* A person might say, "Heinz should not steal the medicine because he will consequently be put in prison if he does." Or, "Heinz should steal the medicine because his wife will die if he doesn't, and who will cook for him then?"
>
> *Stage two (meet your needs):* "Heinz should steal the medicine because he will be happier if he saves his wife." Or, "Heinz should not steal the medicine because prison would be worse than his wife's death." (Moral stages one and two describe the moral reasoning of very young children, though some people never progress beyond this elementary level of morality.)
>
> *Stage three (conformity; "What will people think?"):* "Heinz should steal the medicine because people will think ill of him if he lets his wife die." Or, "Heinz should not steal the drug because people will view him as a criminal if he does."
>
> *Stage four (law and order; follow the rules; legalism):* "Heinz should not steal the medicine because the law prohibits stealing." Or, "Heinz should steal the drug for his wife but also take the prescribed punishment for the crime as well as paying the druggist what he is owed."
>
> *Stage five (social contract):* "Heinz should steal the medicine because our nation recognizes that everyone has a right to life, regardless of the law." Or, "Heinz should not

> Christianity is not unique with regard to moral standards, as we know, but rather is unique regarding how we can satisfy these standards.

---

149 Just as archaeology often gives us more detail about places and events than are recorded in Scripture, so also Kohlberg's research gives us more detail about the development of moral understanding than is given in Scripture. Genuine and objective science complements what we know from Scripture. Knowledge is always the Christian's friend, not enemy.

steal the medicine because the scientist has a right to fair compensation. Even if his wife is sick, it does not make his actions right."

Stage six (universal moral standards): "Heinz should steal the medicine because saving a human life is a higher value than the property rights of another person." Or, "Heinz should not steal the medicine because others may need the medicine just as badly, and their lives are equally significant."[150]

Kohlberg said the highest level of moral reasoning, stage six, is summarized by the Golden Rule: "Do unto others as you would have them do unto you." Kohlberg said that the Golden Rule can also be stated as, "Love your neighbor as yourself." The sixth stage of morality also includes justice and equality before the law.[151]

It is significant that Jesus described the highest level of morality the same way as Kohlberg. Matthew recorded for us the following exchange:

And one of them, a lawyer, asked Him a question to test Him. "Teacher, which is the great commandment in the Law?" And He said to him, "You shall love the Lord your God with all your heart and with all your soul and with all your mind. This is the great and first commandment. And a second is like it: You shall love your neighbor as yourself. On these two commandments depend all the Law and the Prophets." (22:35–40)

This same universal moral code is stated in Leviticus 19:18: "You shall not take vengeance or bear a grudge against the sons of your own people, but you shall love your neighbor as yourself: I am the LORD."

The apostle Paul stated this universal moral code exactly the same way:

For the commandments, "You shall not commit adultery, You shall not murder, You shall not steal, You shall not covet," and any other commandment, are summed up in this word: "You shall love your neighbor as yourself." (Romans 13:9)

Paul also said: "For the whole law is fulfilled in one word: 'You shall love your neighbor as yourself'" (Galatians 5:14).

It is evident, therefore, that Kohlberg's conclusions are largely in agree-

---

150 Many videos are available online that illustrate these moral stages. See, for example, "Kohlberg's Theory of Moral Development," 5:53, posted by Learn To Code, November 22, 2013, www.youtube.com/watch?v=svDYaQUVWfI.
151 These are moral principles, not moral rules.

ment with the Scriptures and Jesus Himself in describing morality. Jesus and the Scriptures understood morality by the knowledge that comes from God. Kohlberg came to his conclusions by means of his pioneering scientific research. He was observing the effects of the moral law as known by nature. These moral precepts, as is evident from Kohlberg's research, are real, observable, and universal. That is, they amount to what we know as natural law.[152] Kohlberg said it this way: "I will present evidence that the factual assumptions made by theories of ethical relativity are not correct; that there are in fact universal human ethical values and principles."[153]

It is unfortunate, however, that Kohlberg did not recognize the existence of God and love for God as being an essential part of the universal moral code. This is a major inconsistency on his part since there can be no genuine morality without including recognition of God's existence and allegiance to Him.

Kohlberg was also wrong in viewing the Ten Commandments as being level four morality. Some interpret the Commandments this way, but doing so is superficial and incorrect. The Ten Commandments and the law of love are two ways of describing the same moral code. The Commandments say by application and rule what the law of love says in principle. How is it that we love our neighbors? We do so, as Luther pointed out in his explanation of the Commandments, by protecting their life, property, marriage, good name, and so forth. Luther explained the Commandments by explaining how they provide the detail on how the highest level of moral principles, the Golden Rule, should be applied to our daily lives.[154]

Kohlberg's research also added some useful detail to how natural law operates. He determined, for example, that only one-third of the population reaches level six moral reasoning. Most people never get beyond level four. Perhaps these two-thirds of the people need the specific rules and applications found in the Ten Commandments because they do not fully understand the law of love—level six. The specific commandments additionally make it more difficult to rationalize away or distort the law of love for those who are at level six.

There are a multitude of practical applications of this

> The Commandments say by application and rule what the law of love says in principle.

---

152 Regarding justice as part of level six moral reasoning, see Acts 17:31 and Luther's comments on justice at the end of this chapter.
153 Munsey, *Moral Development*, 26.
154 As clarified in Luther's Large and Small Catechisms in his explanation to the Ten Commandments.

research, but for our purposes here, we wish to emphasize that Kohlberg's research demonstrates that moral standards are real, singular, and universal. This means that his research provides scientific verification of the reality of natural law. As mentioned above, even the humanists have been convinced of the reality of the universal moral code, likely because of Kohlberg's research—as evidenced by the change of position in their 1980 statement of faith, the wording of which echoes the findings of Kohlberg.[155]

In addition, Kohlberg's research provides us with detail on natural law that can be useful in evangelism, as well as in other endeavors. For example, the research is useful in child-rearing, for it shows parents that they should not expect a two-year-old to respond well to being told he should act in a loving way. Two-year-olds understand pain much better than they understand the Golden Rule.

Kohlberg's work can also help us better understand some of the verbal exchanges between Jesus and His antagonists. These Jewish leaders consistently confronted Jesus with superficial moral judgments while Jesus responded to them with higher-level moral principles. As a consequence, Jesus' antagonists were never sure what had hit them. Jesus explained the doctrinal dynamic behind these dialogues in John 7:22-24:

> Moses gave you circumcision (not that it is from Moses, but from the fathers), and you circumcise a man on the Sabbath. If on the Sabbath a man receives circumcision, so that the law of Moses may not be broken, are you angry with Me because on the Sabbath I made a man's whole body well? Do not judge by appearances, but judge with right judgment.

Jesus' antagonists were judging Him based on legalistic moral reasoning, level four—no work is allowed on the Sabbath. Jesus responded by showing them that they were, first of all, inconsistent in their use of level four moral reasoning, but more important, incorrect in their conclusions by showing them that helping someone in need is a higher moral value than following a superficial interpretation of Mosaic Law. Jesus' enemies were reasoning based on level four morality (legalism). Jesus was following level six and answering His critics based on level six, the law of love. He told His critics they should follow His example. Every recorded accusation by the Jewish leaders that Jesus was breaking the Sabbath follows this same paradigm.

Martin Luther, like Kohlberg, saw level six moral principles as taking

---

155 See the ethics section in *A Secular Humanist Declaration*, 1980.

priority over the other levels of morality. Like Kohlberg, Luther also saw justice as being an essential part of the highest level of moral reasoning, level six. Both observations are evidenced by Luther's comments recorded below:

> This story is told of Duke Charles of Burgundy. A certain nobleman took an enemy prisoner. The prisoner's wife came to ransom her husband. The nobleman promised to give back the husband on condition that she would lie with him. The woman was virtuous, yet wished to set her husband free; so she goes and asks her husband whether she should do this thing in order to set him free. The husband wished to be set free and to save his life, so he gives his wife permission. After the nobleman had lain with the wife, he had the husband beheaded the next day and gave him to her as a corpse. She laid the whole case before Duke Charles. He summoned the nobleman and commanded him to marry the woman. When the wedding day was over he had the nobleman beheaded, gave the woman possession of his property, and restored her to honor. Thus he punished the crime in a princely way.
>
> Observe: No pope, no jurist, no lawbook could have given him such a decision. It sprang from untrammeled reason, above the law in all the books, and is so excellent that everyone must approve of it and find the justice of it written in his own heart. St. Augustine relates a similar story in *The Lord's Sermon on the Mount*. Therefore, we should keep written laws subject to reason, from which they originally welled forth as from the spring of justice.[156]

By this example, Luther made it clear that justice and what he calls the law of "untrammeled reason" (natural law) takes priority over, and is properly the basis of, the laws adopted by governments. One wishes that more of the intellectual and governmental leaders of our time understood these truths equally well.

6. Natural law is attested to by our conscience.

Secular dictionaries have no difficulty defining the word *conscience*. A typical definition will state that conscience is a basic sense of right and wrong that everyone possesses, and a person uses this moral sense as a guide for behavior and will feel guilty when these moral standards are violated. The reality and importance of conscience is widely acknowledged. Arthur Schopenhauer, Immanuel Kant, John Locke, Adam Smith, and Henry David

---

[156] AE 45:128–29.

Thoreau all wrote about our conscience, as have numerous other prominent authors. Untold numbers of artists have attempted to paint it. And each year, the American Society of Journalists and Authors (ASJA) presents the Conscience In Media Award to journalists whom the society deems worthy of recognition for following the highest principles of journalism in the face of personal cost or sacrifice.[157]

Martin Luther often spoke about the role of our conscience and understood it very well. Said Luther:

> Conscience is not a power designed to act but a power designed to judge, one that judges acts. Its proper work is, as Paul says in [Romans] 2:15, to accuse or excuse, to charge with guilt or to absolve from guilt, to make fearful or secure. Its office, therefore, is not to do but to sit in judgment on what has been done or is to be done; this makes a person either guilty or innocent before God.[158]

We frequently hear references to the guilt that is the result of violating one's conscience, just as Luther said would be the case. Model and actress Jennifer O'Neill, for example, has expressed deep regret for having had an abortion; a terrible decision, she lamented, for which she suffered serious consequences of guilt.[159] (Thankfully, Jennifer found forgiveness in the cross of Jesus Christ and is now a tireless worker for the pro-life cause and for the only cure for guilt, that being faith in Jesus, the King of kings.)[160]

In Paul's statement in Romans above, he explained that our conscience bears testimony to the reality of natural law. So it does. Just as there can be no crime in secular courts unless some law has been broken, so with our conscience, there can be no awareness of having done right or wrong without some moral law as a reference point. Similarly, we constantly evaluate our position—how far we have traveled, how much we have eaten, the time of day, and so on, by making reference to a standard of some kind. In the same way, the reality of conscience, either approving or condemning our actions, requires the existence of a moral standard by which moral judgments are made.

---

157 See the following for more information: http://asja.org/For-Writers/ASJAs-Annual-Writing-Awards/Awards-Recipients/Conscience-In-Media.
158 Luther, *What Luther Says*, paragraph 982.
159 Biography of Jennifer O'Neill, at www.jenniferoneill.com. See also the YouTube video "Project Abortion: The Untold Story," May 24, 2017, https://www.youtube.com/watch?v=f0NfswElV5Q&feature=youtu.be.
160 O'Neill, "Project Abortion" (video).

APPLYING NATURAL LAW TO EVANGELISM

An in-depth knowledge of natural law is extremely useful in evangelism and mission work. Perhaps the most important application is that we can engage others with Jesus knowing that the person to whom we are speaking already knows the moral law, whether by nature (instinctive natural law) or instruction of some kind or both. We normally do not need to spend much time convincing someone that the moral law exists, though we may have to explain what it means because of the confusion surrounding morality in our time. We may also have to explain how it applies specifically to the person to whom we are speaking

> There can be no awareness of having done right or wrong without some moral law as a reference point.

People will often rationalize their behavior or distort the moral code in ways that prevent them from seeing that they have personally violated this moral code. Our proclamation of the law should focus primarily on revealing that the person to whom we are speaking has violated it.

For some individuals, it may only be necessary to use biblical quotations such as Romans 3:23, which says: "For all have sinned and fall short of the glory of God." Others, however, may not regard the Scriptures as being authoritative. Are there ways to proclaim God's Law without quoting the Bible?

Jesus clearly did so in His conversation with the woman at the well of Sychar. Jesus mentioned none of the commandments to her, nor did He tell her about the law of love. She already knew all that in her heart. But Jesus did say to her,

> "Go, call your husband, and come here." The woman answered Him, "I have no husband." Jesus said to her, "You are right in saying, 'I have no husband'; for you have had five husbands, and the one you now have is not your husband. What you have said is true." The woman said to him, "Sir, I perceive that You are a prophet." (John 4:16–19)

Jesus didn't have to tell this woman about the nature of promiscuity, and the hyperbole in her comment to the town's people ("He told me all that I ever did" [John 4:39]) strongly suggests that she stood convicted of her sin. She knew instinctively that adultery is wrong (natural law), and she knew she was living in this sin. But Jesus didn't end with Law; He immediately followed this Law with the Gospel. The conversation continued as follows: "The woman said to Him, 'I know that Messiah is coming (He who is called Christ). When He comes, He will tell us all things.' Jesus said to her, 'I who speak to you am He'" (John 4:25–26). Jesus made no references to moral standards, biblical or otherwise. He only described how this woman was living her life, and that was sufficient. In addition, everything He said to this woman pointed to Himself—to the Lamb of God who would take away the sin of the world. Paul followed this same approach at the Areopagus on Mars Hill (Acts 17:22–34), as did Peter in his Pentecost sermon (Acts 2:1–41). We also observe that every missionary sermon recorded in Acts contains three parts—the Law, the Gospel, and evidence to demonstrate that the message is true (apologetics). The overriding focus is always on the Gospel message of the Savior.

In summary, we do well to recognize that morality is not a matter of personal opinion. It's a matter of what objectively exists in the real world. Studying natural law is much like studying the law of gravity—both are critically important features of the natural world God created, and both have a major impact on our lives every day. We may or may not like how these laws affect our lives, but we are powerless to change them in any way. We do well to understand natural law as accurately and completely as possible and adjust our thinking and living accordingly.

We should also recognize that in the missionary presentations recorded in the New Testament, the evangelists spent relatively little time proclaiming the moral law. They didn't need to say very much—their listeners already knew the law because it was written on their hearts. At the same time, however, the moral law, whether understood by being a human or by instruction, prepares people for the Gospel, and in that sense, makes evangelism and mission work possible. It also gives us a much-needed road map for conducting our lives as well as restraining evil to a degree that makes civilized life possible.

> Morality is not a matter of personal opinion. It's a matter of what objectively exists in the real world.

We must always remember, though, that our work as evangelists is effective for one reason and one reason only—it connects lost sinners with the power of God in the glorious message of Jesus Christ. The moral law has no power to save; that power lies only in the Gospel message of Jesus. And this Gospel message contains the same power of God that called the entire universe into existence out of nothing. We can never overestimate the Gospel's amazing ability to bring lost souls into the kingdom of Christ. It's because of God's saving and almighty power in this message of the Savior that we are successful in evangelism and mission work.

QUESTIONS FOR REVIEW AND DISCUSSION

1. Have you heard people make excuses for their immoral behavior? (Perhaps you can think of some excuses you yourself have made.) If so, what were some of those excuses? Which moral levels might be represented by these excuses?

2. Have you ever heard someone say that right and wrong do not exist? How about someone who said, "What's right is what's right for you"? Or someone who said, "It may be wrong for us, but other cultures see this differently"? How might you respond to someone who makes any of these statements?

CONCLUSION AND APPLICATION

One of my seminary students remarked that the information in this book presents a new way of looking at Christianity. That is true, sort of, but at a deeper level, the information in this book actually presents the old way of looking at Christianity. This work follows the model laid down by the apostles and prophets and emulates their manner of proclaiming the Gospel message. What has been said here does not contradict anything we already know. Rather, this content promotes a largely lost dimension that complements what we have previously understood.

SHARING THE FAITH WITH OTHER BELIEVERS

This information provides you, the reader, with effective ways of sharing your faith—including the reason you believe—with others, believers and unbelievers alike. We will begin this section with a description of how this information can give you an open door of opportunity to share the Gospel and the evidence of its truth with those who are, or may be, other Christians. You can begin by presenting them with this question: If someone were to ask you, "Why should I become a Christian instead of a follower of a different religion?" what would you say?[161]

I have posed this question to numerous Christian people. Most of them have great difficulty answering the question. One can see their minds searching their memory files for an answer they believe should be there—but usually it's not. As a result, they say something irrelevant or nothing at all.

Other Christians, albeit a much smaller number, will say something like this: "You should become a Christian instead of a follower of a different religion because Christianity is a religion of faith while other religions are based on good works." A statement like this is true, of course, but it doesn't really answer the question. That can be seen by asking a follow-up question, namely: "But why should people prefer a religion of faith over a religion of works?" This group of people will then usually join the others in not knowing what to say.

At the same time, however, the difficulty Christian people have with this question may not always be a matter of not knowing the answer. It may be that we normally focus on what Christianity teaches, not on whether

---

161 As the reader knows, this book began with the same question.

Christianity is true. The correct answer isn't even on the table. The right answer may be out of sight and out of mind.

Most important, the people searching for answers to your question will want to know how you would answer it. When that happens, you can explain that individuals should become Christians instead of a follower of a different religion because Christianity is true and the other religions are not. You can then add that not only is Christianity true, but there is a wealth of objective, historical evidence that proves it's true. This answer is largely the forgotten and untold secret of our time, and the answer applies to Christianity compared to any and all other religions of the world. Few people know that Christianity is the only religion that can be adequately supported by objective evidence. In our day of skepticism, relativity, and outright spiritual ignorance, this is a truth that people desperately need to hear.

The answer above is the answer the Scriptures have always given when people were called upon to choose between following Jesus or another religious position, or between following the Lord God versus another god. As we have seen, Elijah dealt with a people who were undecided about following God or following Baal. Accordingly, Elijah asked them: "'How long will you go limping between two different opinions? If the LORD is God, follow Him, but if Baal, then follow him'" (1 Kings 18:21). Elijah, then, on Mount Carmel, demonstrated to the people that God is real, while Baal was not (1 Kings 18:23–40). Elijah provided the people with both the correct answer about which god they follow and the objective evidence to demonstrate that this answer was true.

In our time, however, we have largely lost sight of this all-important distinction between Christianity and other religions. We usually don't think or talk along these lines. In addition, it is common in our time for people to believe that there are many different paths to God that are equally true. Isn't it time we get back to the basics regarding the reason people should adopt any religion and explain that there is only one faith that includes adequate reasons for our allegiance, that there is only one faith that is both true and can be known to be true?

SHARING THE FAITH WITH UNBELIEVERS

We can share our faith with unbelievers, or those whom we don't know to be believers, along similar lines. We usually don't need to put them on the spot by asking questions. But it is easy to tell others that the evidence for the truth of Christianity is really strong. It is easy to tell others that the historical evidence that Jesus rose from the dead is truly impressive. When we tell people these important truths, we are telling them something they have almost certainly never heard before. How can we live in a country where Christianity is all around us, but where most people have never heard that there is overwhelming evidence that Jesus has actually risen from the dead and has done so in real physical history? Amazing, but it's true. As a result, it won't appear to others that we are preaching to them when we tell them about the evidence for the truth of Christianity. We will simply be giving them information—information that is new to them and is absolutely fascinating—information that has extraordinary importance for their well-being.

Most people are curious. And most everyone likes learning something new. When we tell others about the evidence for the resurrection, we are appealing to their natural curiosity. We need to be ready to give examples to back up what we say, of course, and that is largely what this book is for. Christians who understand this evidence for the truthfulness of their faith are better equipped to share their faith than those who aren't aware of this evidence. As we have seen, the apostles themselves used evidence extensively in their mission work. They gave their listeners information that was new to them, information explaining and proving that God Himself has visited our planet, and as a result, their problem of sin has been solved. We, like the apostles, can tell others that it really happened—that God has come as the incarnate Son who lived and died in our place so we can be forgiven and restored into fellowship with Him, both in the here and now and forever in paradise. The apostles were sure to include convincing evidence to demonstrate that all they said was true—in particular, that God raised Jesus to life in order to prove that He is the Messiah, the promised Savior of the world. We should do the same; we should describe to others the convincing proof that Jesus really did rise from the dead and that He is alive today. There is nothing anyone can hear that is more important!

SOME WILL BELIEVE; OTHERS WILL NOT

Not everyone will listen, of course. Some will be preoccupied with other things. Others will see the implications that acknowledging the resurrection will have on their lives and be unwilling to believe. Ultimately, we do not know why people decide as they do. But we know that some people will want to know more, and some will heed the message and become believers in Jesus Christ and come into the Kingdom in doing so. We must never underestimate the power of the Gospel message of Christ; as Paul said, "For I am not ashamed of the gospel, for it is the power of God for salvation to everyone who believes, to the Jew first and also to the Greek" (Romans 1:16). The Gospel is powerful because the Holy Spirit uses it to create faith. The Holy Spirit uses this Gospel message, and only this Gospel message, to create a new spiritual life of faith in all those who believe the message. And we remember once again that the power of God's Word in the Gospel of Christ is the same power that called the universe into existence out of nothing.

A FAITH BASED ON EVIDENCE

There will be occasions where we will wish to explain that all competing religions require a blind leap of faith. All other religions ask people to adopt a faith having no objective evidence for its truth. People are being asked to believe something just because someone says they should. We might point out that people normally don't make major changes in their lives without good reasons. Why should they make a blind leap regarding their religious beliefs?

Christianity, in contrast, is based on good and sufficient evidence. The Holy Spirit utilizes history, real and objective history that can be verified in numerous and reasonable ways, to show us that the message is true. God made us to be rational beings, and He utilizes our rationality in reaching us. He does so to show us that we are hearing the truth, real truth. God uses evidence just like an attorney in a court of law uses evidence, just like a debater uses evidence.

The apostle John explained how the use of evidence, the work of the Holy Spirit, and the power in the Gospel message of Jesus Christ all fit together. John said:

> Now there was a man of the Pharisees named Nicodemus, a ruler of the Jews. This man came to Jesus by night and said to Him, "*Rabbi, we know that you are a teacher come from God, for no one can do these signs that you do unless God is with him.*" Jesus answered him, "Truly, truly, I say to you, unless one is born again he cannot see the kingdom of God." Nicodemus said to Him, "How can a man be born when he is old? Can he enter a second time into his mother's womb and be born?" *Jesus answered, "Truly, truly, I say to you, unless one is born of water and the Spirit, he cannot enter the kingdom of God.* That which is born of the flesh is flesh, and that which is born of the Spirit is spirit. Do not marvel that I said to you, 'You must be born again.' The wind blows where it wishes, and you hear its sound, but you do not know where it comes from or where it goes. So it is with everyone who is born of the Spirit."
>
> Nicodemus said to Him, "How can these things be?" Jesus answered him, "Are you the teacher of Israel and yet you do not understand these things? Truly, truly, I say to you, We speak of what We know, and bear witness to what We have seen, but you do not

receive Our testimony. If I have told you earthly things and you do not believe, how can you believe if I tell you heavenly things? No one has ascended into heaven except He who descended from heaven, the Son of Man. And as Moses lifted up the serpent in the wilderness, so must the Son of Man be lifted up, that whoever believes in Him may have eternal life.

"For God so loved the world, that He gave His only Son, that whoever believes in Him should not perish but have eternal life. For God did not send His Son into the world to condemn the world, but in order that the world might be saved through Him. (John 3:1–17, emphasis added)

In these verses, Jesus explained three interrelated processes that must take place for someone to become a member of His kingdom. As they applied to Nicodemus, these are the three processes: (1) Because of the miracles Jesus performed, Nicodemus is convinced that Jesus is a true spokesman, or prophet, of God; (2) for Nicodemus to become part of the kingdom, the Holy Spirit must create a new spiritual life in his heart; and (3) the Holy Spirit creates this new spiritual life by means of the Gospel message that Nicodemus is invited to receive, that being, "For God so loved the world, that He gave His only Son, that whoever believes in Him should not perish but have eternal life." By trusting in this Gospel message, that is, by faith in the Gospel of Jesus Christ, Nicodemus and all others who believe the message are given the new spiritual life that makes them members of God's kingdom.

This is the glorious message that we are asked to bring to the ends of the earth. Nothing is more important! To God be our thanks and praise! Amen.

ANSWERS TO END-OF-CHAPTER QUESTIONS

Chapter 1

Question 1: What if a non-Christian were to ask you why he or she should become a Christian instead of a follower of another religion? What would you say?

Suggested answer: You could say that he or she should become a Christian instead of a follower of another religion because Christianity is true and the other religions are not. This book begins with this question and ends with this question. More detail on the question itself will be provided in the conclusion to the book; information that defends the suggested answer comprises the content of the work as a whole.

Question 2: How do you think the apostle John might have answered that question?

Suggested answer: In his Gospel, John repeatedly emphasizes that his readers should put their trust in Jesus Christ because this Gospel message is true. For example, John records this dialogue between Jesus and Pilate: "Then Pilate said to Him, 'So, you are a king?' Jesus answered, 'You say that I am a king. For this purpose I was born and for this purpose I have come into the world—to bear witness to the truth. Everyone who is of the truth listens to My voice,' Pilate said to Him, 'What is truth?'" (John 18:37–38). John here follows the overarching distinction that the entire Bible makes between Christianity and all other religions—Christianity is true and the other religions, or religious positions, of the world are not.

Chapter 2

Question 1: Why might a pastor be more likely to include apologetics in a sermon given at a funeral than at a regular church service?

Suggested answer: Since funerals and weddings normally attract significant numbers of unbelievers, the pastor has the opportunity to give an evangelistic-style sermon in order to facilitate conversion of these lost souls.

Apologetics is an important aspect of evangelism, and for that reason, pastors will want to use it extensively, especially when non-Christians are in the audience.

Question 2: Christians are sometimes told, "The only reason you are a Christian is because your parents were Christians. If you had been raised a Muslim, you would be one too." How might you respond to this accusation?

Suggested answer: This question should be faced by every adult Christian who was raised in a Christian home, and we should admit that being raised by Christians is not a good enough reason for being a Christian. At the same time, however, this book and others like it make it abundantly clear that there are very good reasons for being Christian, the primary reason being that Christianity is true and can be proven to be true. No other religion can make this claim. For this reason, the accusation above is a devastating critique of all religions—except Christianity.

CHAPTER 3

Question 1: Various opinion polls suggest that as our knowledge of the universe grows, the percentage of our population who believe in God declines. Why might this be?

Suggested answer: The aggressive promotion of Darwinism in our schools and elsewhere has had the effect of convincing large numbers of people that God does not exist. It is the promotion of this atheistic worldview that is responsible for the increase in atheism and agnosticism, not the advancement of scientific knowledge.

Question 2: Traditionally, science has been defined as obtaining knowledge by means of observation. Today, however, science is often defined from the viewpoint of philosophical naturalism, also called materialism, the view that the universe consists of nature plus nothing—nature is all there is. Not surprisingly, those who define science this way end up concluding that God does not exist and adopting evolution because, as they see it, the alternative (special creation) is impossible. As Christians, how should we deal with this new definition of science?

Suggested answer: We should point out that the new definition of science is not a legitimate definition at all, but instead is an unverifiable and philosophical assumption of atheism.

Chapter 4

Question: 1: Can you think of a way the criteria for identifying true prophets could have been improved? What additional criteria should have been added?

Suggested answer: It is difficult to imagine how these criteria could be improved.

Question 2: Are those who say they don't believe the Bible actually taking a blind leap of faith away from Christianity? How might you respond to someone who says this?

Suggested answer: Those who say they don't believe the Bible, in most cases, are taking a blind leap of faith. It is actually worse than that—they are taking a leap of faith that is contrary to all the evidence. They should be directed to the question of Jesus in Matthew 15:16 ("Who do you say that I am?") and be invited to read how Peter answered that question as well as how the other Gospel writers answered the question.

Chapter 5

Question 1: We have seen from statements by C. S. Lewis that he, too, was a masterful teacher. Yet he did not generate the kind of opposition that Jesus did. How might we account for this difference?

Suggested answer: Lewis didn't claim to be God.

Question 2: What would you say are some of the qualities of good teachers? Do these qualities fit Jesus of Nazareth? Why or why not?

Suggested answer: The most important quality of a good teacher is pursuit of the truth; others include being knowledgeable, having a passion for the instruction of one's students, being a good communicator, being willing to challenge popular opinions, being honest and straightforward and not a manipulator, being fair, and being willing to sacrifice for the sake of the truth.

Actually, we can describe the qualities of Jesus of Nazareth and the qualities of a good teacher and our descriptions will be one and the same. The conclusion that should be drawn from this realization is obvious: Jesus was the master teacher.

Chapter 6

Question 1: It is not unusual for people to say, "I don't believe in miracles, the reason being that I've never seen one." How might you respond to someone with that viewpoint?

Suggested answer: I would direct him or her to chapter 10 in this book, to the section describing the Shroud of Turin. I would then explain why the only reasonable explanation for the image on the shroud is that it was formed in a miraculous way. The key is that the image on the shroud not only appears to be miraculous, but also portrays the message of the cross. And it's this message of Jesus Christ crucified and raised—the Gospel message—that has the ability to bring people to faith.

Question 2: Some people say, "We don't even know if there ever was a Jesus of Nazareth." Is that a reasonable statement? How might you respond to someone who says this?

Suggested answer: You should explain that it would be difficult to find any credible historian who agrees with that statement because the historical evidence for the existence of Jesus is overwhelming. You might add that if we don't know that Jesus lived, then we don't know if Socrates lived, or Aristotle, or even Alexander the Great, because the evidence we have for Jesus is at least as good, or better, than for any of these other historical figures. Then invite them to consider some of the evidence that Jesus lived in real history and invite them to consider what Jesus did for us on the cross.

Chapter 7

Question 1: How might someone try to explain the similarities between the messianic prophecies and Jesus' life and death without concluding that Jesus is the promised Messiah?

Suggested answer: It is difficult to see how this could be done in a reasonable way.

Question 2: We have seen that the promise of the coming Messiah is the unifying theme of the entire Old Testament. What do you think is the unifying theme of the New Testament?

Suggested answer: The unifying theme of the New Testament is that the promised Messiah has come in the person of Jesus of Nazareth. Jesus now invites all people everywhere to repent of their sins and put their trust in Him so they can live in fellowship with Him and inherit eternal life in His presence as well.

Chapter 8

Question 1: The story is told of a man who wanted to start a new religion. An acquaintance of his told him, "Jesus of Nazareth died and rose again to found His religion; you could do at least as much." Does this story illustrate an important difference between Christianity and the other religions of the world? Explain. See also Isaiah 41.

Suggested answer: Jesus paid the ultimate sacrifice in order to establish His religion and the Church, His Bride. He also provided the best possible evidence of its truth by His resurrection from the dead. No other religion can claim anything like this.

Question 2: How does knowing for certain that Jesus rose from the dead influence the way that you see death?

Suggested answer: We will see in the next two chapters that the lives of the disciples were totally changed when they saw the risen Jesus. Seeing Him risen from the dead caused these disciples to have no fear of death. They knew that they would be raised just as Jesus had been raised. We have this same assurance of His resurrection and our own. One of the purposes of this book is to allow you, the reader, to see Jesus. You will not see Him in exactly the same way the apostles saw Him, but you can see Him in a very real sense, nonetheless. The power of the Holy Spirit allows you to see Him in His Word and Sacraments. You will see Him in one of the artifacts pictured in Chapter 10. And you will see Him as He sees you in chapter 13.

CHAPTER 9

Question 1: Consider the Jewish leaders who tried to find an explanation for Jesus' healing of the man born blind. How does that view compare with the view of skeptics today who deny the resurrection of Christ?

Suggested answer: We can't generalize about everyone, of course, but at the same time, those living now who deny the resurrection, for the most part, do so for the same reason that Jesus' enemies wouldn't accept Him as the Messiah. They simply refuse to believe. It is not a matter of some being worse sinners than others, some being more closed-minded, or the like. It's nothing like that at all. Jesus clarified this matter in His parable of the wedding banquet (Matthew 22:1–14). This parable explained that everyone is invited to the banquet. Some people accept the invitation and attend the banquet; others refuse to attend. Why do some accept the invitation to attend the banquet, to be part of God's kingdom, while others do not? This is a question Scripture does not answer. We simply do not know. (Freedom, even limited freedom, by its very nature cannot be explained.)

Question 2: How can we equip our young people with a working knowledge of apologetics before they go off to higher education or the workforce?

Suggested answer: The first big hurdle is for parents and the Church to decide that they are willing to do what is necessary to equip our teenagers with adequate knowledge of apologetics. If this instruction doesn't happen, not only will our youth be ill-equipped for sharing their faith, but many, if not most, will leave the Church and not come back. These teens are often being taught in school and by the culture that how they feel about something is more important than whether it is true. They are being taught that the Bible is unreliable and that Darwinian evolution has been proven to be accurate. For the most part, the Church has not equipped our youth to deal with these heresies. Our teens need to know that we have very good reasons for trusting the integrity of the Bible, and we have very good reasons for believing that the Gospel message is true. Our teens need to know the information in this book and other books like it. God willing, you, the reader, can play an important role in bringing this about.

Chapter 10

Question 1: Did you notice the striking similarity between the image on the shroud and the various paintings of Jesus of Nazareth? How might this similarity be explained?

Suggested answer: Actually, the paintings of Jesus made before the fourth century AD bear no similarity at all to the image on the shroud. Beginning in the fourth century, however, the vast majority of paintings and other works of art depicting Jesus are remarkably similar to the image on the shroud. They reveal this likeness in numerous and striking details. This observation has led many scholars to conclude that awareness of the shroud likely became widely known in the fourth century, and artists from that time forward then used this image as their model for their art. As time went on, artists used fourth century and later artworks, which were originally based on the shroud, for their models. The evidence for this view appears to be quite strong.

Question 2: The apostle John tells us that right after Jesus raised Lazarus from the dead, "many of the Jews therefore, who had come with Mary and had seen what He did, believed in Him" (John 11:45). Do you think the apparent resurrection pictured on the shroud could have a similar effect in our time? Why or why not?

Suggested answer: The image on shroud does continue to have this effect. The shroud clearly portrays the message of the cross, and the message is this: "The power of God for salvation to everyone who believes" (Romans 1:16). As mentioned in this chapter, for example, several members of the scientific team that studied the shroud (members of the Shroud of Turin Research Project, or STURP) converted to Christianity because of the image on the shroud. Prior to their study, all members of the team were skeptics who were convinced that they would quickly discover how the image had been forged, and that would be that. The research team was amazed (shocked might be a better word) to find no scientific explanation that could even begin to explain the image and said as much in its report. Several members of the STURP team have subsequently devoted their lives to continued study of the shroud (See Wilson and Schwortz, *The Turin Shroud*, as well as other scholarly works on the shroud.)

Chapter 11

Question 1: Do any other religions depict the Almighty as a God of love and grace "who desires all people to be saved and to come to the knowledge of the truth" (1 Timothy 2:4)? Explain.

Suggested answer: No other religion sees God as being gracious and loving to the point of sending His Son to live and die on our behalf, as one who would, because of what His Son has done, declare the whole world to be forgiven (objective justification). In addition, Christianity is the only religion that recognizes God as completely righteous and holy, a God who is always morally good and promotes only that which is good. Christianity is additionally the only religion that includes adequate proof for its truthfulness.

Question 2: If God is a loving God, why does He allow evil and suffering to exist in this world that He created?

Suggested answer: See chapter 12 of this book.

Chapter 12

Question 1: Jesus referred to His Church as His Bride. What does that say about the way He sees us?

Suggested answer: It is difficult to imagine how Jesus could have used a more powerful description to portray His relationship with us, a relationship described by His servant Paul as follows:

> Husbands, love your wives, as Christ loved the church and gave Himself up for her, that He might sanctify her, having cleansed her by the washing of water with the word, so that He might present the church to Himself in splendor, without spot or wrinkle or any such thing, that she might be holy and without blemish. In the same way husbands should love their wives as their own bodies. He who loves his wife loves himself. For no one ever hated his own flesh, but nourishes and cherishes it, just as Christ does the church, because we are members of His body. "Therefore a man shall leave his father and mother and hold fast to his wife, and the two shall become one flesh." This mystery is profound, and I am saying that it refers to Christ and the church. However, let

each one of you love his wife as himself, and let the wife see that she respects her husband. (Ephesians 5:25–33)

Question 2: What is the greatest act of love?

Suggested answer: "'Greater love has no one than this, that someone lay down his life for his friends'" (John 15:13).

Chapter 13

Question 1: Additional artworks of ancient peoples that picture dinosaurs are being discovered even today. At least fifty such works of art are now available. The mainline media seems to ignore these discoveries for the most part. In contrast, every so often a new "missing link" in the history of man is discovered, only to be dismissed as a false lead a few years later. How can this double-standard be explained?

Suggested answer: It appears the Darwinian evolutionists and their defenders are rather desperate to find key missing links. This is especially true for any such links connecting dinosaurs to birds and linking primates to human beings. The difference between dinosaurs and birds, and between apes and men, are so huge, however, that many missing links are required, not just one or two. None have been found that stand up to critical examination. Because the needed missing links have not been found, some evolutionists now speak of giant, inexplicable leaps forward, for which there is no evidence. Some Darwinists now say that the missing links will never be found because they do not exist, so another theory is required. Science itself is not the issue. The driving force behind Darwinism is unbelief—the religious view that we don't need God to explain the creation of the universe, and we can't trust the Bible to tell us what is true.

Question 2: As mentioned earlier, John Sanford's work demonstrates that natural selection cannot substantially improve a living kind, nor can it bring about new kinds. Why might secular science want to ignore what he says?

Suggested answer: Sanford's position of genetic entropy (deterioration) of the genetic code can easily be observed, especially as it relates to human beings. But once again, scientific knowledge is not the issue. Unbelief in the form of materialism (there is no God) is the crux of the matter.

Chapter 14

> Question 1: Have you heard people make excuses for their immoral behavior? (Perhaps you can think of some excuses you yourself have made.) If so, what were some of those excuses? Which moral levels might be represented by these excuses?

Suggested answer: Common excuses include "Everybody does it," "I am sure he means well," "I'm not hurting anyone," "Don't impose your moral values on me," and many others. These excuses are almost always moral levels one through four, and usually levels one and two. People are merely finding excuses for doing something they want to do for their own perceived benefit.

> Question 2: Have you ever heard someone say that right and wrong do not exist? How about someone who said, "What's right is what's right for you"? Or someone who said, "It may be wrong for us, but other cultures see this differently"? How might you respond to someone who makes any of these statements?

Suggested answer: One way to penetrate through this moral relativism or outright denial of morality is to tell people a parable and ask for their response. Here is a parable that may be useful:

In the year 2000, a movie was produced called *Cast Away*. It portrayed the struggles of a man (played by Tom Hanks) marooned on a small island all by himself. Now, what if there had been two people so marooned, a man and a woman? And what if the man, because he was bigger and stronger than the woman, decided to force her into essentially being his slave? Would that be okay?

Since it is difficult for people to hold that slavery is, in principle, perfectly fine, your audience is likely to say that slavery is not okay. If so, they have admitted that universal moral standards do exist. Such standards do not depend on governmental laws, and they are simply there whether we admit to them or not.

Kohlberg found that when confronted with a moral situation, people will invariably appeal to a moral standard of some kind for guidance. It is not possible to even discuss moral situations without appealing to moral standards. Even "might makes right" is a moral standard, albeit a deficient one.

"If it feels good, do it" is a moral standard, albeit a poor one. It may be useful to point out that even the humanists couldn't maintain their denial of universal moral principles.

At the same time, as a matter of principle, we should not lead people to a conviction of having violated the moral law without explaining to them the Gospel message of the cross. The moral law will drive people to despair; the cross can transform them into being members of the glorious kingdom of the risen Lord, Jesus Christ. And this is what apologetics is all about.

BIBLIOGRAPHY

Altman, Rochelle I. "Official Report on the James Ossuary." *The Bible and Interpretation*. Accessed July 7, 2017. www.bibleinterp.com/articles/Official_Report.shtml

American Humanist Association. "Humanist Manifesto II." American Humanist Association, 1973. https://americanhumanist.org/what-is-humanism/manifesto2/.

American Museum of Natural History. "The Problem of Size." Accessed July 6, 2017. www.amnh.org/exhibitions/dinosaurs-ancient-fossils-new-discoveries/theropod-biomechanics/the-problem-of-size/.

Anchor Bible Dictionary, vol. 1. New York: Bantam Doubleday Dell Publishing Group, Inc., 1992.

Antonacci, Mark. *The Resurrection of the Shroud*. New York: M. Evans and Company, Inc., 2000.

Babylonian Talmud: Tractate Sanhedrin, Folio 43a. Come and Hear: An Educational Forum for the Examination of Religious Truth and Religious Tolerance. Accessed May 17, 2017. www.come-and-hear.com/sanhedrin/sanhedrin_43.html.

Behe, Michael J. "Irreducible Complexity Obstacle to Darwinian Evolution," 2004. Accessed June 30, 2017. www.lehigh.edu/bio/Faculty/Behe/PDF/Behe_chapter.pdf.

Blaiklock, E. M. *The Archeology of the New Testament*. Grand Rapids, MI: Zondervan, 1970.

Bruce, F. F. *The New Testament Documents: Are They Reliable?* Grand Rapids, MI: Eerdmans, 1960.

Brug, John. "The Origins of Earth and People." *Northwestern Lutheran* 86, no. 12 (December 1999): 32.

Charles, J. Daryl. Foreword to *Natural Law: A Lutheran Reappraisal*. Edited by Robert C. Baker et al. St. Louis: Concordia, 2011.

Crabtree, Vexen. "The Problem of Evil: Why Would a Good God Create Suffering?" Last modified December 13, 2016. www.vexen.co.uk/religion/theodicy.html.

Craig, William Lane. "The Problem of Evil." *Reasonable Faith*. Accessed July 6, 2017. www.reasonablefaith.org/the-problem-of-evil.

Darwin, Charles. *The Origin of Species by Means of Natural Selection: or the Preservation of Favoured Races in the Struggle for Life*. New York: Avenel Books, 1968.

Dawkins, Richard. Quoted in Gregg Easterbrook, "Science and God: A Warming Trend?" *Science* 277, no. 5328 (August 15, 1997): 890–93.

———. *River Out of Eden: A Darwinian View of Life*. New York: Basic Books, 1995.

———. Twitter, January 7, 2015, 6:55 a.m., https://twitter.com/RichardDawkins.

Declaration of Independence: A Transcription. Last updated January 19, 2017. Accessed May 17, 2017. www.archives.gov/founding-docs/declaration-transcript.

Dostoevsky, Fyodor. *The Brothers Karamazov*. USA: The Easton Press, 1979.

Driver, Rebecca. "Sea Monsters . . . More than a Legend?" *Creation* 19, no. 4 (September 1997): 38–42. Reprinted at Answers in Genesis, https://answersingenesis.org/dinosaurs/dragon-legends/sea-monsters-more-than-a-legend/.

Ehrman, Bart. "Biblical Views of Suffering." *The Bart Ehrman Blog*, March 8, 2013. https://ehrmanblog.org/biblical-views-of-suffering.

Fields, Helen. "Dinosaur Shocker." *Smithsonian Magazine*, May 2006. Accessed July 6, 2017. www.smithsonianmag.com/science-nature/dinosaur-shocker-115306469/?no-ist.

Geisler, Norman. *Christian Apologetics*. Grand Rapids, MI: Baker, 1976.

Habermas, Gary. "The Resurrection Evidence That Changed Current Scholarship," YouTube video, 1:14:30, from To Everyone an Answer: 10th Annual EPS Apologetics Conference. Posted by Biola University, September 14, 2013. www.youtube.com/watch?v=5znVUFHqO4Q.

———. "The Resurrection Argument That Changed a Generation of Scholars," YouTube video, 1:20:42, from The Veritas Forum at the University of California, Santa Barbara. Posted by The Veritas Forum, November, 8, 2012. www.youtube.com/watch?v=ay_Db4RwZ_M.

Habermas, Gary, and Michael Licona. *The Case for the Resurrection of Jesus*. Grand Rapids, MI: Kregel Publications, 2004.

Horgan, John. "Pssst! Don't tell the creationists, but scientists don't have a clue how life began." *Scientific American*, February 28, 2011.

Josephus, Flavius. *The Works of Josephus*. Translated by William Whiston. Lynn, MA: Hendrickson Publishers, 1980.

Jupp, Peter. "Piri Reis Map of Antarctica—Antarctica Ice Free!" *Ancient Destruction Blog*. Published July 14, 2012. www.ancientdestructions.com/piri-reis-map-of-antarctica.

Kohlberg, Lawrence. "The Philosophy of Moral Development: Moral Stages and the Idea of Justice." *Essays on Moral Development*, vol 1. Edited by Lawrence Kohlberg. San Francisco, CA: Harper & Row, 1981.

Lee, Adam. "4 Beneficial Evolutionary Mutations That Humans Are Undergoing Right Now." Accessed May 17, 2017. http://bigthink.com/daylight-atheism/evolution-is-still-happening-beneficial-mutations-in-humans.

Lewis, C. S. *Mere Christianity*. New York: MacMillan, 1960.

Luther, Martin. *Luther's Works: American Edition*. Volumes 1–30: Edited by Jaroslav Pelikan. St. Louis: Concordia, 1955–76. Volumes 31–55: Edited by Helmut Lehmann. Philadelphia/Minneapolis: Muhlenberg/Fortress, 1957–86. Volumes 56–82: Edited by Christopher Boyd Brown. St. Louis: Concordia: 2009–.

———. *What Luther Says: A Practical In-Home Anthology for the Active Christian*. Compiled by Ewald M. Plass. St. Louis: Concordia, 1959.

Mahoney, Tim. *Patterns of Evidence: Exodus: A Filmmaker's Journey*. St. Louis Park, MN: Thinking Man Films, 2014. DVD.

———. *Patterns of Evidence: Exodus*. St. Louis Park, MN: Thinking Man Films, 2015.

Maier, Paul. *Jesus: Legend or Lord?* 8-part series, available from Lutheran Visuals, www.lutheranvisuals.com. DVD.

———. "The Real Jesus: Paul Maier presents new evidence from history and archeology at Iowa State," YouTube video, 1:28:19. Posted by The Veritas Forum, May 11, 2013. www.youtube.com/watch?v=XAN3kQHTKWI.

Munsey, Brenda, ed. *Moral Development, Moral Education, and Kohlberg*. Birmingham, AL: Religious Education Press, 1980.

National Institutes of Health. "What Is a Genome?" National Institutes of Health: US National Library of Science. Published July 5, 2017. https://ghr.nlm.nih.gov/primer/hgp/genome.

New World Encyclopedia, s.v. "Sodom." Last modified October 9, 2015. www.newworldencyclopedia.org/entry/Sodom.

Newport, Frank. "In U.S., 42% Believe Creationist View of Human Origins." Gallup, June 2, 2014. www.gallup.com/poll/170822/believe-creationist-view-human-origins.aspx.

———. "More Than 9 in 10 Americans Continue to Believe in God." Gallup, June 3, 2011. www.gallup.com/poll/147887/americans-continue-believe-god.aspx.

———. "Most Americans Still Believe in God." Gallup, June 29, 2016. www.gallup.com/poll/193271/americans-believe-god.aspx.

Newton, John. *Olney Hymns*, vol. 1. Hymn 99. 1779. www.musicanet.org/robokopp/english/howkindt.htm.

Noebel, David. *Understanding the Times: The Religious Worldviews of our Day and the Search for Truth*, 2nd edition. Irvine, CA: Harvest House, 2006.

Nohl, Frederick. *Luther: Biography of a Reformer*. St. Louis: Concordia, 2003.

Nye, Bill, and Ken Ham. *Uncensored Science: Bill Nye Debates Ken Ham*, produced by Answers in Genesis, 2014. DVD.

Owen, James. "Oldest Living Tree Found in Sweden." *National Geographic News*. April 14, 2008. http://news.nationalgeographic.com/news/2008/04/080414-oldest-tree.html.

Parton, Craig. *The Defense Never Rests*, 2nd edition. St. Louis: Concordia, 2015.

Petrovich, Douglas. "The Battle for the Bible and Why It Is So Important." Lecture given in Eden Prairie, MN, March 23, 2017.

Plantinga, Alvin. *God, Freedom and Evil*. Grand Rapids, MI: Eerdmans, 1978.

Quist, Allen. *Many Convincing Proofs: A Biblical Approach to Christian Apologetics*. Mankato, MN: Lutheran Synod Book Company, 2008.

———. *Ten Truths about Evolution That Everyone Should Know*. 2014.

Richardson, Michael et al. "There Is No Highly Conserved Embryonic Stage in the Vertebrates: Implications for Current Theories of Evolution and Development." *Anatomy & Embryology* 196, no. 2 (August 1997): 91–106.

Roberts, Alexander, and James Donaldson, eds. *The Ante-Nicene Fathers: Translations of the Writings of the Fathers down to A.D. 325*. Revised by A. Cleveland Coxe. Edinburgh: T. & T. Clark. Reprinted Grand Rapids, MI: Eerdmans, 1996.

Rosenbladt, Rod. "Are You Prepared to Give a Defense? A Crash Course in Evidential Apologetics," *Modern Reformation* 2, no. 3. (May/June 1993).

Sanford, John. *Genetic Entropy & the Mystery of the Genome*, 3rd edition. Waterloo, NY: FMS Publications, 2008.

Scott, J. Julius. "Did Jerusalem Christians Flee to Pella?" Paper presented at Archaeology Conference, Wheaton College, Wheaton, IL, 1998. The Preterist Archive, accessed July 5, 2017. www.preteristarchive.com/Bibliography/1998_scott_flee-pella.html.

Sereno, Paul. "SuperCroc." *National Geographic*. Published September 2008. Originally published December 2001. http://ngm.nationalgeographic.com/2008/09/supercroc/sereno-text/3.

Stein, Ben. *Expelled: No Intelligence Allowed*. Directed by Nathan Frankowski. Universal City, CA: Premise Media Corporation, 2008. DVD.

Strobel, Lee. *The Case for Christ: A Journalist's Personal Investigation of the Evidence for Jesus*. Grand Rapids, MI: Zondervan, 1998.

———. *The Case for Christ: The Film, A Journalist's Personal Investigation of the Evidence for Jesus*. Directed by Michael Eaton and Timothy Eaton. Santa Monica, CA: Lion's Gate Films, 2007. DVD.

Tacitus. *Annals*, book XV, paragraph 44. *The Complete Works of Tacitus*. Edited by Moses Hadas. Translated by Alfred Church and William Brodribb. USA: Random House, 1942.

Tackett, Del. *Who Is Jesus? Building a Comprehensive Case*. Produced by Focus on the Family's *The Truth Project*. Carol Stream, IL: Tyndale House, 2013. DVD.

Thayer, J. H. *Greek-English Lexicon of the New Testament*, 4th edition. New York: Charles Scribner's Sons, 1901.

Veith, Gene Edward, Jr. *Postmodern Times: A Christian Guide to Contemporary Thought and Culture*. Wheaton, IL: Crossway, 1994.

Wells, Jonathan. *Icons of Evolution: Science or Myth*. Washington, DC: Regnery Publishing, 2000.

Wilson, Clifford. "Ebla: Its Impact on Bible Records." *Acts and Facts* 6, no. 4 (April 1977). www.icr.org/article/ebla-its-impact-bible-records.

Wilson, Ian, and Barrie Schwortz. *The Turin Shroud: The Illustrated Evidence*. London: Michael O'Mara Books Ltd., 2000.

Yahya, Harun. "The Irreducible Complexity of Wings Refutes Evolution." Published 1994. Accessed May 17, 2017. www.harunyahya.com/en/Darwinism-Watch/147852/the-irreducible-complexity-of-wings.

Zacharias, Ravi. "The Problem of Suffering and the Goodness of God—Ravi Zacharias at Johns Hopkins," YouTube video, 1:58:56, from The Veritas Forum at Johns Hopkins University. Posted by The Veritas Forum, December 21, 2013. www.youtube.com/watch?v=t7-gP1gC8gM.

SCRIPTURE INDEX

OLD TESTAMENT

GENESIS
1:1...35
1:3...68
3:2–3...125
3:15...74
14:2...53
17:4–8...75
21:12...75–76
22:18...75
49:10...76

EXODUS
3:8...75
4:1–5...44–45
14:13–31...20
14:30–31...41

LEVITICUS
19:18...162

NUMBERS
24:17–19...76

DEUTERONOMY
13:1–5...47
18:15–18...99
18:15–20...47
30:15–20...49–50
34:10–12...45

JOSHUA
2:8–14...41
2:11...41–42
3:7–17...45–46
6:1–20...53
6:24...53

2 SAMUEL
22:9...145

1 KINGS
17:17–24...70
17:24...44
18:21...171
18:20–40...42–43
18:23–40...171

2 KINGS
4:32–36...70
17:7–8...50n33

2 CHRONICLES
18...51

JOB
1:8...126
19:25–27...128
38:4...127
40:15–24...141–142
41...143–145
41:15–17...145–146

PSALMS
16:8–11...77
19:1–4...30
22:1–18...78–79
34:20...81
110:1...82

ISAIAH
7:14...80
9:6...79
11:1–6, 10...76–77
41...100, 179

53:4–6...83
53:7...81
53:9...82
53:12...81

JEREMIAH
23:5–6...77
23:13...51
23:14...51
28:9...49

EZEKIEL
13:8–9...51–52

DANIEL
5:22–31...49
7:13–14...82

JOEL
2:16–21...19

MICAH
2:11...51
3:5...51
5:2...50, 80

ZECHARIAH
9:9...80
11:12–13...81

NEW TESTAMENT

MATTHEW
1:18...80
2:4-6...50
5:31-32...48, 62n43
11:20-24...72-73
12:9-14...63
12:22-29...14
16:15...120, 177
16:16...118, 120
19:3...48
19:3-9...61-62
19:8-9...48
19:19...60
19:20...60
22:1-14...180
22:35-40...162
24:2...85
26:15...81
27:5, 7...81
27:12-14...81
27:46...129
27:57-60...82

MARK
2:10...82
15:27...81

LUKE
1:1-3...101
1:1-4...104n70
1:30-35...80
7:22-23...65
10:25...61
10:25-37...58
13:4-5...127
13:34...15
16:31...15, 99
19:35-38...80
21:20-24...85

23:34...81
23:53...113
24:25-27...84

JOHN
1:1...79
1:1-3...70
1:3...68
1:4...68
1:9-16...79
1:29...119
2:18-22...22, 88
3:1-17...173-174
3:1-21...126n103
3:3-8...13
3:16...129
3:16-17...120
3:19-20...14-15
4:10...119
4:16-19...167
4:19...20, 46
4:25-26...167
4:39...167
7:5...97
7:22-24...164
8:10...119
9:1-38...65-67
9:17...46
9:28-29...68
9:29-33...46
9:32...67
9:32-33...68
11:25-26...99
11:38-44...14
11:38-53...69
11:39...70
11:45...118, 181
11:48...14, 47
12:17-18...71

12:18...12
15:13...183
15:26-27...103
18:14...47
18:37-38...175
19:23-24...79
19:30...119
19:33, 36...82
19:35...101
20:6-7...115
20:26-28...22
20:30-31...12, 13

ACTS
1:3-5, 8...96
1:4-5...104n71
1:18-19...17
1:21-22...17, 104
2:1...17
2:1-41...168
2:2-15...18-19
2:16-21...19
2:22...20, 72
2:22-23...20
2:24-32...21
2:30-32...77-78
2:32...23
2:33-41...23-24
3:15...70
4:13...96
5:34-39...94
13:12-21...97
16:16-18...48n32
17:22-31...25
17:22-34...168
17:30-31...88
17:31...163n152
18:12-17...106
18:28...83

20:27...150
26:26...52, 72
26:27-29...74

ROMANS
1:16...12, 117, 172, 181
1:19-20...29
1:20...157
1:21...156
2:14-15...32, 151, 152, 153
2:15...150, 157, 158, 159-160, 166
3:23...126n105, 167
4:22-25...88-89
5:12...125-126
8:7...126
8:28...128
8:37-39...128
13:9...162

1 CORINTHIANS
9:1...104n69
15:3-24...89-90
15:5-8...12
15:6-7...97
15:7-9...104n69
15:8...101

GALATIANS
1:11-12...104n71
1:18-19...111
3:16...75
5:14...162

EPHESIANS
2:8-9...13
5:25-33...182-183

PHILIPPIANS
4:3...92

HEBREWS
1:3...82
11:3...38, 39

1 PETER
3...12
3:15...11

2 PETER
1:16...12
1:16-18...101
1:16-21...54
1:19...51, 85n51
1:21...54
2:4...126

1 JOHN
4:1...56

REVELATION
21:3-5...129

ABOUT THE AUTHOR

Allen Quist is adjunct professor of Apologetics at Bethany Lutheran Theological Seminary, Mankato, Minnesota, and is also a member of the Committee on Doctrine for the Evangelical Lutheran Synod. He was professor of Religion and Psychology at Bethany Lutheran College from 1968 to 1981. In 1981, he was elected to the Minnesota House of Representatives, where he served three terms from 1982 until 1987. He served as chair of the Social Services Subcommittee and vice-chair of the Human Services Committee. While in the House, Quist was the author of numerous bills and amendments. He was chief author of the bill that created Minnesota's Department of Jobs and Training, replacing the old Department of Economic Security. Quist was also chief author of the bill that led to the legalizing of homeschooling in Minnesota.

As a researcher, Quist uncovered the extraordinary marriage penalty hidden in the Affordable Care Act (Obamacare). The results of his research were widely publicized in a variety of national venues. The prestigious Heritage Foundation used Quist's work as the starting point of its own research and exposé on the marriage pealty. In addition, Quist has authored seven previous books.

Allen Quist's primary interest and area of research, however, is in Christian apologetics. He has published three previous books on this topic and has written numerous magazine and journal articles in this field as well. While serving as a professor at Bethany Lutheran College, Quist taught a course in apologetics called "The Case for Christianity." In 2014, he was one of two featured speakers at the Bjarne Wollan Teigen Reformation Lectures on the topic of Christian apologetics.

Quist holds a master of arts degree from Minnesota State University, Mankato, and a bachelor of divinity degree from Bethany Lutheran Theological Seminary, Mankato, Minnesota. He and his wife, Julie, live in rural St. Peter, Minnesota. They have ten children and forty-six grandchildren.